1926

Homicide in America

This copy has grammar and spelling errors.
they have been corrected in later printings

David Kulczyk

1

SWELL DAME PRESS

The information in this book is true and complete to the best of the author's knowledge. It is offered without guarantee on the part of the author. The author disclaims all liability in connection with the use of this book. Do not disturb the occupants of any of the addresses listed in this book.

All rights reserved. No part of this book may be reproduced or transmitted in any form whatsoever without prior written permission from the author except in the case of brief quotations embodied in critical articles and reviews. Podcasters must cite this work if they tell any part of this book on their podcast.

Cover photo by Phil D'Asaro

Dedication

This book is dedicated to John Ballor

1956 – 2019

A gentle, talented soul who played the guitar

just like a bat out of hell

Acknowledgments

I would like to thank April Moore, Joan Renner, Phil D'Asaro, Paul Drexler, J'aime Rubio and Caitlin Rother for being my crime comrades. I also want to thank Time Tested Books (Sacramento), Theo Dzielak, Michael Perry, Jen Picard, Rebecca Perry Damsen, Bill Foreman, Marilyn Sterrett, John Massoni, Richard Sinn, James Van Ochten, Jaguar Bennett, Tara Gellman, Melissa Wolfmann, Monica Stark, William Burg, Jackson Griffith, Michelle Camarda, Hector Nunez, Lisa Nunez, Jerry Perry, and Kristeen Young. And, as always, I want to thank my wife Donna for giving me the time, space and patience to do this book.

Introduction

If you watch or listen to the news media, you would think that we are living in the most violent times in history. But statistics prove that crime has dramatically decreased over the last forty years. But why does it seem like crime is out of control? The 24-Hour news cycle has the media scrambling for stories, so what 30 years ago would have been a local story about a mother killing her child is now international news.

It is easy to forget that our great-grandparents faced death every day. Horses and mules killed people as much as cars do now. They cooked with wood, kerosene, or coal burning stoves that were accidents waiting to happen. They drove cars that had zero safety features, guaranteeing death at the slowest of speed. Getting an infection was a death sentence. People murdered, kidnapped, and raped in the same horrible ways before mass communication as they are nowadays. They often got away with their crimes back then too. Life was cheap in the old days.

The 1920's was a time of massive cultural and technological changes. The death and destruction of World War I dope-slapped the collective mindset of the youth of America. Four million earnest young men signed up or were drafted by the United States for what they thought was a war for God, glory and honor, and instead found a world of shit.   For the first time in U.S. history a rich person could not buy a substitute to fight for him. The families of the rich and the poor sent their sons off to fight in a nasty war. They dreamed of god and glory and found guts and gory.

Millions of young men, most who had never been farther than ten miles from their family home before the war, came back from Europe. Not only had they experienced the calamity of war, they had made friends with other young soldiers. Men, who would have never had the opportunity to meet people of other ethnicities, and religions, became comrades in wartime. Old prejudices were forgotten in the trenches, or while on-leave in Paris. The young men understood they were the ones dying for a war that was in sense, a royal family feud.

When the smoke cleared over thirty million human beings were dead from combat or the effects of the war. Compounding the misery, a deadly strain of influenza spread rapidly across the globe in 1918, killing an estimated fifty-million people. The pandemic killed primarily young and otherwise healthy people. It killed quickly, usually three days after the first symptoms. Victims died drowning in their own blood.

There were reminders of the Great War that had ended for all to see. Men with missing legs hobbled down the street on crutches. Other not so lucky, wore life-like masks to hide what was left of their faces after being hit in the face with a bullet, shrapnel or the rifle stock of a German Mauser. Others lingered in sanitariums waiting for their bodies to finally give out.

The war and pandemic affected everyone, young and old, rich and poor. Everyone suffered. The array of death and injuries rendered the restrictive Georgian moralities hollow. Most of the world's youth had seen death personally, and they realized that it is a fragile thing, and too important to live according to the rules of Puritans elites.

If the disaster that was World War I and the 1918 Flu Pandemic ripped the corsets and veils off the old ways, the Nineteenth Amendment to the Constitution, gave American women the right to vote and a new-found voice. The long-fought battle for the right seemed to strip women of the silently enforced code of behavior that was proper since the Victorian Age. More females entered the workforce, with a "can do" attitude. Married women started to stand up to their husbands and demanded more say in the way things were done at home. Young single women put off marriage and got their own housing, moving away from their domineering parents.

If that was not shocking enough for the older people, young women started to smoke cigarettes in public, wear cosmetic makeup, drink alcohol, and not only patronized speakeasies, but they patronized them without a male escort. Women and men performed animated dances like the Charleston and the Brown Bottom to jazz music at all night drunken parties.

At the movie houses the youth saw actors living carefree and exciting lives and decided that the hypocritical sexual morals of their parents were no longer relevant. They all wanted to be aloof, fun loving or mysterious like Clara Bow, Theda Bara, John Gilbert or Rudolf Valentino. The youth movement of the 1920's had no official name. The media labeled the females "flappers," and later the decade was tagged, "the Roaring Twenties."

The Volstead Act of 1919 led by conservative Protestants was a thinly veiled anti-Catholic movement that made alcohol illegal. Because laws against fun are never popular, underground nightclubs called speakeasies popped up everywhere. Hundreds of books have been written about Prohibition, so I would like to point out that illegal clubs made nightlife more exciting. The thrill of being allowed into an exclusive place just to have a drink was exhilarating for the youth of the day.

Ordering a drink which was usually watered-down booze or homemade semi-poisonous gin was like gambling, it might be good, or it might be bad. Dancing and gambling usually took place in the speakeasies adding to the excitement and danger.

A number of things caused the world to become a smaller place by the 1920's. The advent of affordable automobiles combined with improved motorways enabled people to cover distances in an hour, that just a decade before took an entire day.

The nation also got smaller when National Broadcast Company, yup, NBC, started scheduled nation-wide radio broadcasts in 1926. Suddenly everyone with a radio could listen in real-time with everyone else in the country. The shared experience ranging from fishermen out at sea, to a lone teenager out in the middle of nowhere, to residents of large cities. Young and old, rich or poor, everyone shared the same audio event. Radio was only made available to the public for less than a decade. This was an extraordinary leap in human awareness.

I feel that coast to coast radio caused a subconscious epiphany of an amazing future, especially among the youth. It also served as an omen to some who feared a world that they could not or would not adjust to. The swift cultural and scientific surge destroyed careers and a way of life for many.

1926 was the year that Americans all over the country said screw it. And screw it they did... mixing too much bootleg booze, marijuana, cocaine, and heroin, with fast cars, sex, and jazz music can only lead to trouble. The number of allegedly normal people senselessly committing ghastly murders in 1926 is astounding. It is like a switch got turned on and some people went mad unlike any other time in American history.

Table of Contents

He Otto Stayed Home

August 3, 1926

Chilo, Ohio

67

Like a Girl That Married Dear Old Dad

August 6, 1926

Springfield, Massachusetts

69

Really Bad Dad

August 14, 1926

New Richmond, Ohio

72

Darn those Socks

August 20, 1926

Carter Lake, Iowa

75

Jitney Bill's Café

August 22, 1926

San Jose, California

78

The Cozy Café

August 22, 1926

Shambaugh, Iowa

80

Author's Note

This book came about while I was working on my previous five books on murder and death. I notice a lot of homicides happened in 1926. Not only was there a jump in homicides, the murders that occurred in 1926 were extraordinarily violent and personal. Over the years I have made notes of murders that occurred in 1926 and stashed them away in my files for later.

In 2016 I started working on this book. In the meantime, I published *Forgotten Sacramento Murders 1940-1976* in 2018. When it came time to publish, my usual publisher rejected it. As did several other publishers. I finally did get a publisher, but our relationship did not blossom, instead they wanted to change my writing style, and the very essence of this book. I got out of the contract and decided to release it myself. I hope you enjoy this chronology of violence during the good old days.

The Farmer in the Dell?

January 19, 1926
Clinton, Pennsylvania
Murderer – Hart Reed
Victims – Palmer Reed / Irma Eaton

In 1926 Clinton, Pennsylvania was a rural backwater crossroad. Twenty-odd miles west of Pittsburgh, the only way to get there was via unimproved dirt roads that were muddy most of the year. Most of the residents who lived around the Allegheny County village in 1926 were farmers.

Hart Reed was a twenty-two-year-old religious fanatic, who worked his family farm about a mile west of Clinton, near Raccoon Creek State Park. On January 19, 1926, Reed burst into the kitchen of the family home where Hart's forty-five-year old mother Palmer Reed, his married sister Irma Eaton and her two infant children were passing time. Reed pounced upon his mother and sister with a butcher knife, immediately inflicting severe wounds. Bleeding profusely, the pair managed to escape to the basement root cellar, locking the door behind them.

Reed, covered in his family's blood, sat down on the steps leading to the cellar, waiting for his mother and sister to make an escape. Reed did not pay attention to his screaming niece and nephew a few feet away from him.

Hearing the commotion, handicapped farmhand, Emmett Lytle entered the house and was immediately attacked by Reed. They fought in the gore covered kitchen, until Lytle made a break for the barn.

When Dewar Reed and his son Ambrose arrived back to the farm from doing errands, Lytle ran to the men and told them what he had seen. Being the older brother, Ambrose was used to dealing with his brother's tantrums, but he had no idea just how serious his brother's outburst was this time.

Reed had thrown up barricades, blocking doors and windows into the farmhouse. Ambrose pleaded with his brother to let him in. After tiring of his brother's refusals, he broke in through a window, and after a vicious fight he subdued his brother on the blood smeared floor and tied him to a chair.

Ambrose heard the women screaming and found them near death on the dirt floor of the dank cellar. Before they died, they told him what had occurred.

Reed was not finished with his rampage, and got loose from his ties, grabbed his knife, and ran out of the house across a frozen field towards neighbor Robert Crawford's place. Reed started a fire in Crawford's barn and ran off into the nearby woods. The barn filled with hay and straw burned quickly and was a total loss.

Crawford formed a posse with his neighbors and ran down Reed, who put up a great fight until he was clubbed on the head with a fence post. It took hours for the police to make their way over the muddy roads to pick up their murderer.

On January 22, 1926, the court found Hart Reed insane, and committed him to the State Asylum for the Criminally Insane in Fairview, where he apparently spent the rest of this life.

I Love a Man in a Uniform

January 20, 1926

New Castle, Pennsylvania

Murderer – Dorothy Bertha Pegran

Victim – Sargent Phillip Tulley-U.S.M.C.

In 1926, New Castle, Pennsylvania was a prosperous little city ten miles east of the once important industrial city Youngstown, Ohio. Jobs were for the taking at the nearby limestone quarries, fireworks factories or for the Pittsburgh and Lake Erie Railroad. Immigrants from southern and eastern Europe moved there to take advantage of the early 20th Century industrial explosion.

With all the prosperity that New Castle enjoyed, the United States Marine Corps needed to jazz up their recruitment in the busy city. Peace is bad for the military, and America was still sleeping off the hangover from the Great War. The good paying jobs hurt recruiting to the point that the Marine Corps were offering bonus money for reenlistments. Joining the military was low on the list of opportunities in western Pennsylvania.

Marine Sargent Phillip Tulley of Pittsburgh took the Marines up on the offer. The tall, handsome, and charming forty-year old veteran was the ideal poster boy for recruiting. His first assignment after re-upping with the Corps was New Castle, just fifty-six miles northwest Pittsburgh.

Sargent Tulley and his thirty-three-year-old wife Dorothy made the easy two hour move on January 16, 1926, taking two adjoining rooms at a boardinghouse owned by Margaret Winters at 205 North Mill Street. Tulley's recruiting office was inside the New Castle City Hall, where his good looks and smart uniform must have impressed more than a few women who worked there, because just three days later, Miss Winters took a phone message from a woman for Tulley.

Phillip came home around eleven in the evening that night and Dorothy confronted him in their bedroom about the call, and where he had been, but Tulley laughed it off. As the night wore on, they argued more intensely.

Their landlady slept through the entire argument, until she was awoken by a bleeding Sargent Tulley, who stumbled into her unlocked bedroom around one in the morning and fell on her floor, moaning. Dorothy charged into her room, knelt next to Tulley and kissed him gently, telling him to get up and come back to bed. Tulley stumbled with Dorothy back to their room. The stunned Winters then heard three gunshots. She quickly called the police.

The police and ambulance arrived to find the couple laying over each other on the blood covered floor. When the attendants looked at their wounds, they discovered that most of the blood belonged to the Marine. Dorothy's wound was superficial. They were taken to Shenango Valley Hospital where Phillip Tulley died a few hours later.

The Marine Corp was informed and Tulley's commanding officer was on the first train to New Castle, but before he left, he notified Tulley's "next of kin." Dorothy was bandaged up and taken to the Lawrence County jail.

Dorothy was beside herself with grief. She wept uncontrollably in her cell. The sheriff and his wife, who was the jail matron, took pity on the woman, who spoke freely to them about her crime and her love for the Marine sergeant.

"I never loved a man in my life like I did Sergeant Tulley," she was quoted. "And when you love a man like I did him. You just can't tell what's liable to happen. I wouldn't care if they could chloroform me, but I don't want to be electrocuted. I want to be freed of this charge of murder they have against me, but life isn't ever going to be the same for me after this."

Dorothy was correct as later that day, a woman with an eight-year old son showed up to claim the Marine's body. She said her name was Nan Tulley and she had been married to the Sergeant since August 20, 1917. The young boy with her was their son, Phillip Junior, and they lived in Pittsburgh.

Dorothy was livid with Nan and Junior's arrival, telling the Sherriff, "Don't give her anything! Don't let her have the body. She's not his wife. She was married to some man down in New Jersey and never divorced."

4

Even though Nan Tulley could not produce a marriage certificate, Tulley's body was turned over to her for burial at Arlington National Cemetery.

When she was asked about their unusual marriage arrangement, she rationalized melodramatically. "She came to him! Oh, why did he not tell me of that other woman? I would have gone to her and if I found that he cared more for her than me, why I would have given him up. His suffering is over, but hers is yet to come."

Despite numerous requests, the identification of the mystery woman was never revealed. The police responded that they had questioned her and decided that she was not involved in the murder. Locals knew that she was an employee of the city and worked at city hall, where the Marines had their recruitment office. She allegedly left New Castle right after the murder with the blessing of the police.

Dorothy Bertha Pegran went on trial on March 9, 1926, with Judge R. Lawrence Hildabrand presiding over a standing room only courtroom. Nan Tulley showed up in black veils, and little Junior was dressed in a child's Marine uniform. The sordid tale of lost love and jealousy made the trial the must-see event of the year. The courthouse took on a circus-like atmosphere.

Assistant District Attorney Thomas W. Dickey presented his evidence to an all-male jury. Witnesses included Margaret Winters, who told the jury of Tulley bursting into her room and collapsing. She testified that Tulley moaned to her, "my God, call the police. My wife shot me." Winters also told about the mysterious female who had been calling the house and leaving messages for the Sargent.

New Castle police officer C.C. Dickey, who was not related to the district attorney, was the first officer at the crime scene attested to what Margaret Winters told the judge and jury he found the couple on the floor of their room, in a big pool of the sergeant's blood. The Sargent told him that Dorothy shot him.

Dorothy Pegran, who sobbed almost constantly while the prosecution made its case, took the stand in her defense to a hushed courtroom. She told how she fell in love with Tulley, and that they had secretly lived as husband and wife for two

5

years in Pittsburgh. Tulley promised to marry her someday, and Dorothy was happy with the arrangement.

On the night in question, Pegran told the court that Tulley had arrived home hours later then he said he would be, so she had questioned Tulley about the woman who kept calling the house. They argued, and when they both reached for the loaded revolver on the nightstand, Pegran got to it first. After that she claimed that she did not remember anything.

District Attorney Dickey was full of questions for the thirty-three-year-old Pegran. She had already admitted to bigamy, and murder, so it is somewhat confusing why the assistant D.A. decided to needle the hapless woman with personal questions.

Dorothy Pegran was born poor in Dothan, West Virginia. One of nine children, she had a scant education and was barely literate. She could add a little, but not subtract. When she was fifteen or sixteen, she could not remember, she left home to live with iron worker Ernest Tucker. She met Tucker while he was working on an iron railroad bridge near Dothan. He was almost thirty, she was fifteen or sixteen.

When the bridge was finished, Dorothy moved with him to Pittsburgh. She never saw her family again and did not know if any of them were alive or dead. Tucker's occupation involved working away from home, and Dorothy was often left alone in the city that British biographer James Parton called "hell with the lid off."

In the early 1900's, Pittsburgh was the center of the American steel industry and was the ninth largest city in the United State. It was a polyglot of Eastern European immigrants and African Americans who fled the south to work at the steel mills. With foundries running twenty-four hours a day, it had the most polluted air in America.

The D.A. peppered Dorothy with questions about her family, her religion, and her apparent disregard for moral laws placed in the legal books by straitlaced Protestant activist politicians. She answered the insulting questions honestly, between sobs and real tears.

6

On March 12, 1926, the jury deliberated for three hours and came back with the verdict of "not guilty." District Attorney Dickey's vicious cross examination only made the jury feel sorry for Dorothy, and they felt that she was honest in telling her story. Sargent Tulley was a womanizer who had tainted the uniform of the Marine Corps.

Dorothy Pegran was released from jail, but because she had no money or place to live, the sheriff and his wife invited her to stay with them in their home until she could raise some money. The good people of New Castle took up a collection and Dorothy Pegran got on a train to Pittsburgh.

A Moron with a Gun

January 30, 1926

Springfield, Missouri

Murderer – Clinton Hollingsworth

Victims - Joseph Harjung / Detective Albert Franklin

With a name like Clinton Hollingsworth you would think that person would be an Oxford graduate of royal blood, who spends long weekends on the polo fields of Eton. The Clinton Hollingsworth in this story grew up middle-class in Springfield, Missouri, and was, as diagnosed by experts at the time, a moron.

His parents, John and May once said that Clinton Hollingsworth was never quite right, even as an infant. On November 19, 1923, he shot himself in the chest with a .25 caliber handgun. The bullet went into his spine, leaving him paralyzed from the waist down. His father found a suicide note that rambled about a black-haired teenager that he had a crush on.

It took a year before Clinton got out of the hospital. The doctors told John and May their son would never walk again, however Clinton managed to start walking on his own around the beginning of 1926. He also fell down a lot. Although it is not noted at the time, it is possible that Clinton was addicted to morphine and other opiates, and he may have relieved his anguish to the point where he did not feel any pain at all, allowing him to walk

Clinton filed an insurance claim for disability, but the insurance company fought the claim, stating that the policy did not include self-inflicted disability. Depositions were taken where Clinton told the assembled attorneys that he could not remember what happened. The case slowly churned through the legal system.

On January 31, 1926, May and her ten-year old daughter Dolly were spending the afternoon playing rolls on their recently purchased player piano. Clinton came into the living room and seemed to enjoy the tune. Allegedly, Clinton wanted to hear the song again, but was overruled by Dolly and May. Clinton retrieved a 35-30 Savage rifle that his father had recently purchased through a mail order company and walked into the living room. As fast as he walked in, Dolly and May walked out and hid out by their woodshed.

After a half hour, John came home from his job, and May ran up to tell him that Clinton had a gun. As John walked up the driveway to speak to his son, Clinton open fired on his father, hitting him in the palm of his left hand. A man driving by gave the wounded man a ride to the hospital.

Neighbor Joseph Harjung heard the commotion and upon seeing the armed and crazed young man, the twenty-eight-year-old married father of two, turned to run away. He took a 35-30 round in the back of his neck, killing him instantly. When the police and an ambulance showed up the twenty-year old Hollingsworth open fired on the vehicle, wounding the driver and attendant and scattering the bystanders.

Springfield Police Detective Albert Franklin escaped the volley and took cover. When he motioned to the ambulance crew to run towards him, he unknowingly stepped into Hollingsworth line of fire. The detective took a bullet in the chest fired from fifty yards away.

Neighbors grabbed their guns and joined the police who had surrounded the home and for the next three hours, hundreds of bullets were fired into the house by the police and private citizens. Hollingsworth, who was an expert shot, fired over a hundred rounds, going from window to window shooting accurately enough to make the assembled piecemeal posse to keep their heads down.

Finally, after three hours, the police had had enough of the lone shooter. The electric company cut the power to the neighborhood, and the night was lit by flares.

As a diversion, dynamite was thrown into an open crawlspace blowing a hole in the home's floor. At the same time, Constables Jim Cummings and Sam Herrick stormed the house, finding Hollingsworth standing next to the bullet-ridden player piano, holding his rifle. Constable Cummings shot Hollingsworth in the left thigh. He was taken into custody, driven to the hospital, where he was treated for his flesh wound, before police locked him up in the Greene County jail.

9

Hollingsworth relaxed in his jail cell and enjoyed the attention that he was receiving from law enforcement, the prosecutor and the media. The Sheriff of Greene County allowed groups of curiosity seekers to stare at the prisoner as he lay on a cot in this sparse cell. Strange as it sounds, it was not out of the ordinary in 1926. The sightseers were brought in, in groups of thirty to forty people. This human zoo only lasted a few days, as the non-stop traffic of gawkers disrupted the jailhouse routine.

Police questioned Hollingsworth about the gun, where he got it and why was it not registered. He calmly told authorities that his father had bought it through a mail order gun shop. He told police that he had ordered three more guns, but he did not have the money to pay the C.O.D. cost. Police went to the post office and located the packages that were being returned. They contained semi-automatic pistols.

Because Hollingsworth was a known troubled soul, Dr. George A. Johns of Jefferson City and Dr. T. H. Romeiser of the state hospital at Saint Joseph were called in to examine the young killer. Both were considered expert Alienist, what is now the fields of psychiatry or psychology.

The doctors interviewed Hollingsworth's parents, who told them that Clinton was nutty since he was a toddler. They listened to the murderer talk about his morphine use and how he could not remember anything when he was under its influence. He told the doctors that he had taken twenty-five grains of morphine that day and had no memory of the three-hour gun battle. After giving Hollingsworth a battery of test, and observing him for hours, concluded that Hollingsworth was insane.

Dr. J.W. Williams, the Greene County health officer told the media that he concluded that, "the defendant is mentally irresponsible, defective, and with the mind of a child of twelve or fourteen-year old, or what is known as a moron. The prisoner cannot differentiate between right and wrong." When asked if a person in the condition of Hollingsworth shot a man would he know what he was doing?

10

Williams replied, "He would know what he was doing, but would have no conception of the results."

Greene County Prosecuting Attorney Harold Lincoln thought differently and made his opinion clear. "I do not accept the theory that he is crazy," said Lincoln. "I believe he may have taken drugs and that his actions were due to the fact, but his does not relieve him of responsibility for his killing two men and wounding three others."

On March 23, 1926, a jury acquitted Clinton Hollingsworth of first-degree murder on the grounds of insanity. He was ordered to a state mental hospital and ordered to never be at large again.

In 1964, the court allowed the now partially paralyzed fifty-eight-year-old Hollingsworth to leave the hospital grounds to go on a chaperoned fishing trip. Joseph Harjung would have been sixty-five years old in 1964. He never got to go fishing during his retirement.

A Pocket Full of Bullets

March 18, 1926

Stockton and Galt, California

Murderer – Marion John Goin

Victims: Alexander Marengo / Matilda Marengo / Mary Dutra / Carroll McNoble / Florence Podesta / Minnie Podesta

William and Narcissus Watkins Goins welcomed their baby boy, Marion John Goins into the world on February 3, 1877, in Laurel County, Kentucky. He served in the military during the Spanish- American War and ended up in California.

On June 15, 1901, Goins married Cora Proctor in Tuolumne County and they had four children; Alma, Lawrence, Grace, and Clarence. Goins got a job with the Southern Pacific Railroad, starting out as a brakeman, rose to engineer, and eventually becoming a supervising engineer in the Oakland railyards.

Not an easy person to get along with, Goins often quarreled with his co-workers and neighbors. Despite the good job on the railroad, Goins wanted more. He longed to be an entrepreneur but lacked the start-up capital. Goins conceived a fiendish plan. He took out several insurance policies on himself and on October 4, 1911, after loosening a handhold on a Southern Pacific passenger car, he purposely fell off the steps while departing the train in Lodi. His left foot slipped under the train's wheels, severing it at the ankle.

Accidents and deaths were common occurrences among railroad workers, but the Southern Pacific Railroad, a corporation known for their criminal mistrust of their employees, did not like to offer compensation for job-related injuries. And the railroad smelled a rat when Goins filed a lawsuit against them. Both sides had a team of attorneys, and nearly four years later, on September 28, 1915, the case went in front of a judge.

The railroad attorneys blew holes in Goins' story. They accused him of committing fraud to collect on his purchased insurance policies over the loss of his foot. Defense witnesses claimed they saw Goins loosening the handrail on the coach moments before the accident.

Experts examined the handrail and testified it was in fine condition with no signs of wear that would cause it to break. The defense presented questions as to why Goins, who had an employee pass to ride any S.P. train, had purchased a ticket for his trip to Lodi.

The defense claimed that Goins wanted to be seen at the station to back his story. In the end, Goins lost the case and had to pay court costs and attorney fees. The insurance companies, perhaps wanting to avoid a long and expensive judicial battle, issued Goins the payout.

With his newfound financial independence, Goins bought and sold property and businesses from Stockton to Chico. At one time or another, he owned a farm outside of Lodi, a ranch near Placerville, a restaurant, gas station, and a laundry. Described as having an "unbridled temper, unrelenting anger and a vindictive disposition," he was quick to sue anyone who fell behind on payments or had crossed him in real or imagined ways.

He kept a black, leather-bound book in which he wrote the names of people who he felt had crossed him. It was not unusual for Goins to show acquaintances his list, and commenting he'd someday seek revenge on them.

The year 1924 proved pivotal for John Goins. His home in Chico mysteriously burned to the ground. His insurance company suspected arson and refused to pay. Around the same time, Goins got into a heated and public argument with Chico City Attorney J. Oscar Goldstein.

Goins' long-suffering wife, Cora, filed for divorce, but died on the 24th of August, just as the divorce proceedings started. No record exists of Goins collecting money on this wife's death, but it doesn't seem farfetched to believe he had her life insured.

Goins moved to Stockton, leaving his two school-aged children, Grace and Clarence, in boarding school. His older son, Lawrence, had just graduated from high school in Chico, and took a job on a Butte County ranch, while his daughter,

Alma, taught school in the East Bay.

Goins tended to his various business dealings in the Central Valley, moving to Stockton to watch over his latest investment, a gas station in Stockton. He soon met and married forty-six-year old Florence Podesta, the daughter of an Italian immigrant who developed into a prosperous fruit farmer. The marriage did not start off well. Without consulting with his new bride, he bought a home in Stockton for them to live in. She hated the house and refused to move in. Florence liked living in the large, beautifully furnished, family farmhouse at 4224 West Lane Street, complete with a cook and housekeepers. Compared to the farmhouse, the little tin roof home at 114 South Stanislaus Street was a dump.

Florence's married sister, Dora De Paoli managed the trust that included the Podesta farm. Unlike the rest of the men who married into the Podesta family, Goins had no interest working in the family business and living an exceptionally good life with a big and loving Italian family. However, he has great interest in the family bank accounts, something that caused a lot of friction in the family. Goins preferred to turn a fast buck with investments, while a large family farm like the Podesta's, had to make long range financial plans. Dora stood fast and held the leger close.

The pressure built on Goins as his delicately assembled finances started to crumble. The bank over-extended his line of credit for the house he built for Florence and creditors began demanding payment. One business had put a lien on his home for non-payment of services.

On March 16, 1926, John Goins' brain bubbled over with anger and resentment. He set out to right the wrongs he felt had been dealt to him. Jumping into his Dodge sedan, he drove to the Podesta ranch with a .45 caliber pistol and a pocket full of bullets.

Once there, he ran into the house and went down into the basement kitchen where Florence and her married sister, Minnie Clark, were preparing the noon meal. Vera Johnson, the family cook was in the nearby coal house when she heard Goins shout, "I'll get you, Florence," followed by three gunshots. Johnston

14

then heard Goins shout, "I'll get you, Minnie!" followed by another three gunshots. Johnson hid in a nook near the kitchen fearing for her life, as Goins ran past her without noticing. He bumped into farmhand Joe Silva in the doorway. Goins pointed the barrel of his .45 at Silva and muttered, "Keep going." Other farmhands, some of them related to the Podesta family, heard the commotion but were too far away to intervene.

Goins drove into downtown Stockton and entered the law offices of McNoble and Arndt. Attorney and former president of California Bar Association, George McNoble had represented Goins in court to secure his army pension. McNoble had won the judgment and Goins received twenty-five dollars a month. McNoble befriended the businessman, but he had also counseled Florence about hers and Goins' impending divorce.

The staff was preparing to leave for their lunch break when Goins burst into the office. After being informed that McNoble was at a conference in San Francisco, Goins drove to McNoble's home at 403 West Flora Street.

Mary Carroll McNoble stood in the kitchen making lunch when Goins knocked on their door. Nine-year-old John answered and told Goins that his father was not home. Goins curtly asked for Mrs. McNoble.

Annoyed at the disturbance, Mary opened the door to speak with the ill-mannered man. Goins pushed his way into the house and confronted her.

"Did my wife tell George that my house was an old tin can, and she wouldn't live in it?" Goins demanded.

"I don't know anything about my husband's affairs," Mary replied.

"Is that true?" Goins asked.

"Yes. Why did you come here?" Asked the frightened woman. "I don't know anything about it."

"Is that so?" Repeated Goins.

"It certainly is," she said. "What do you mean coming here and questioning me about your wife?"

15

"This is why." Goins pulled out the .45 caliber revolver, stuck the barrel into Mary's chest and pulled the trigger. The hammer landed on an empty chamber with a resounding click. Mary turned to run, but before she took a step, Goins shot her three times in the back. Goins escaped in his sedan while Mary bled out on the floor of her sitting room in front of her young son.

Goins drove north to Lodi, a farming town sixteen miles from Stockton up Highway 99. Around one o'clock, he nervously ate lunch at the Lodi Hotel, then stopped at a gas station on Palm Avenue to check the air in the tires. Witnesses saw him speeding north out of Lodi.

Alexander Marengo and his forty-eight-year old wife Matilda had come to the Sacramento Valley village of Galt not long after arriving in America. Their hard work and perseverance paid off with a successful vineyard and a large, loving family. The Marengo's and Goins' shared a property line in the early 1920s, and despite an incident involving a missing horse, they had a friendly relationship.

Around three in the afternoon, Goins stopped at the Marengo's farmhouse on the east side of Galt. The Marengo's welcomed him into their home, serving him a glass of wine. After an hour of visiting, Goins asked Alexander if he could have a jug of wine to take with him. When Marengo told him told him no, Goins pulled out his .45 and shot Alex and Matilda dead.

Visiting daughter, twenty-seven-year-old Mary Dutra screamed as she tried to make a run for it and was shot three times in the head. Goins ignored Dutra's children, three-year-old Isabella and two-year-old Joe as they screamed. Goins jumped into his car and sped away.

The farmhands working at the Marengo vineyard heard the gunshots. Sons Joe and August Marengo, as well as Dutra's husband Antone, who worked at a neighboring farm all heard the gunshots and screams, but they were too far away to do anything about it. They could only watch the Dodge sedan turn north at the end of the driveway.

Due to his multiple business dealings, Goins was a well-known figure along Highway 99. The murders shocked the normally quiet and mostly rural area. They also knew about Goins' black book and wondered if the unfortunate victims had ended up on the list prior to their cold-blooded murders.

Every police and sheriff's department in the Central Valley were on high alert. They set up roadblocks and called in axillary police. The telephone company mass-called police departments in the area to alert them to the spree-killer.

After driving northeast on Highway 88 to Ione, he arrived in Slough City at 6:00 p.m. where he bought ten gallons of gasoline. Goins asked the station attendant for directions to Placerville and if he had to go through Sacramento. Apparently unaware of his location, Goins was already forty miles east of Sacramento.

Goins disappeared for the next two hours. The police grew anxious believing Goins escaped the dragnet and had made into the Sierra Nevada Mountains, where he could hole up indefinitely.

Goins had stopped at an old friend, Joseph Windle's ranch outside of Diamond Springs. Windle, unaware that every police officer for a hundred square miles was looking for his friend, asked Goins to stay for dinner. Windle noticed Goins disheveled appearance and agitated state. He knew of Goins' marital problems, and let his friend blow off some steam.

"I'm a ruined man," Goins told Windle. "I have lost my all. I don't care if I don't live until morning. My wife's family is against me and has caused me lots of trouble."

Goins left Windle's ranch around 8:30 p.m. and drove toward Diamond Springs, where he was immediately recognized by El Dorado County Supervisor W.S. Biggs, and El Dorado Traffic Officer Slatterback.

Slatterback jumped into his vehicle and sped off after the killer, with Biggs following in his own car. Slatterback had his lights and siren wailing as he chased Goins who had backtracked toward the town of El Dorado. About three miles west of that town, Slatterback and Biggs caught up with Goins and both firing their service revolvers at him. Slatterback pulled alongside Goins, the Dodge went off the road, rolling over on its roof. As Slatterback and Biggs approached the crashed vehicle, they saw Goins' body. A massive amount of blood flowed from

17

his mouth. John Goins, the murderer of six innocent people had stuck the barrel of his .45 into his mouth and pulled the trigger.

As thousands of Californians breathed a sigh of relief, the police speculated that Goins was driving to a ranch he had once owned outside of Placerville. He sold the ranch three years earlier but had difficulty with the purchasers. He was unaware the property owners had moved few weeks before.

Police suspected Goins planned to then confront a former neighbor of the ranch who accused Goins of harboring an illegal still on his property. It appeared that if Goins had the ammunition, he was bent on killing as many people who were in his black book as possible.

Stockton police combed through Goins' belongings at his home and found two rambling letters addressed to his son, Lawrence, informing him to pay off his bills, and to take care of his two dogs, Rover and Beauty.

The next week the dead were buried, and the funerals were attended by hundreds of mourners. John Goins' body was cremated. There were no mourners or funeral.

Like a Hole in the Head

March 21, 1926

Hammond, Indiana

Murderer – Lester C. Simpkins

Victim – Lucile Myers

Lester C. Simpkins was a shadow of his former self. Educated at Valparaiso University in Civil Engineering, he had once been a good provider for his growing family. Along with his wife Anna, and their three children, they traveled wherever Lester's engineering skills were needed.

Anna died while giving birth to their fourth child leaving him a widower with young children. It was not long before Lester met and married Harriet Stone in Lexington, Kentucky and they soon started having children.

Something happened to Simpkins around 1922. He became disinterested with his career and spent most his time fishing and getting a suntan. In 1924, while living in Harvey, Illinois, a violent dispute with a neighbor resulted in Simpkins spending a couple of weeks in jail.

The next year the family moved ten miles east to Hammond, Indiana, where Simpkins continued his life of leisure. To make ends meet, Simpkins' older children worked menial jobs around the Indiana Harbor area of East Chicago.

Word got around that the family was not doing well. A social worker stopped by their home at 417–17th Avenue in Hammond and found that there was not one piece of furniture in the house. The family was given some second-hand furniture and food by a social welfare association.

In late March 1926, someone tipped off the Hammond Police Department about the dire living conditions at the Simpkins house. Harriet was in the hospital after having a hard birth with their sixth child together, making it a grand total of ten children, with the eldest being nineteen. Money was so tight that Lester sold his surveying equipment.

Hammond Police handed over the complaint to Lucile Myers, the Chief Probation Officer for Lake County Juvenile Court. The fifty-one-year-old Myers was an energetic leader in many causes in Lake County. She was the original President of the Lake County League of Women Voters and the first President of the Indiana Association of Probation Officers. Myers was also the Vice Chairperson of the Lake County Republican Party, and the President of the Hammond Welfare Association. Her husband was the deputy treasurer of the city of Hammond, until he shot himself in the head at his office at Hammond City Hall in 1924. Together they had four children.

Myers was overworked. She had a backlog of cases to investigate but found time in her busy schedule to make a welfare check on the Simpkins' home at five in the evening on March 21, 1926. Myers' son William drove her to the home and waited in the car while his mother carried on her business.

Simpkins was not happy to have a probation officer checking up on their welfare. The world-weary Myers was slightly appalled at the squalid living conditions in the home, but she sat herself down in only chair in the house and pulled out her notebook. Seven of the children were home; the other three were out working. Myers started asking or everyone's name and age. When one of the older children started to volunteer the information,

Simpkins got angry and yelled, "Keep your damn mouths shut. If there is any talking down around here, I'll do it!"

Simpkins pulled a pistol out of his pocket and shot the social worker in the right temple. The bullet passed through a decorative buckle on her hat and went clean through her head. Myers slumped over in the chair as the children screamed. Simpkins ran out the backdoor into the chilly twilight. Fourteen-year old Margaret Simpkins ran to a nearby gas station to call the police.

William Myers was completely unaware of the horror that happened inside the house. He saw a man, who turned out to be Simpkins, run from the back of the house, but he did not think anything about it. William finally caught on to the situation when the police showed up with light flashing and

20

sirens blaring.

Police in northern Indiana and southern Michigan were on high alert to find Simpkins, but he was nowhere to be found. Hammond police believed that he had committed suicide.

According to Simpkins family lore, Lester contacted his son Carl in 1938. He and his family met Lester at a farm near Battle Creek, Michigan. Years later, Carl went back to the farm and found it a burnt-out ruin. He questioned neighbors and was told that the farm had burned down years ago. Lester Simpkins had left the area shortly after the fire and was never seen again.

The End of the Frontier

March 25, 1926
Bridger, Montana
Murderer – D.A. Hollowell
Victim – Emma Kerckel

Union County Montana is about as far out in the boondocks as a person could possibly wish to be. Sitting on the bottom center of the state, with Yellowstone National Park as its southern neighbor, the stars are bright at night. In 1926, Union County was still a very western frontier type of place. The Code of the West prevailed strongly there.

Most people would consider forty-two-year old rancher D.A. Hollowell, a lucky man. He had lived in Montana's high country for seventeen years and had much to show for it. His Sand Creek ranch was nestled in the short hills eight miles southwest of Bridger, Montana where he raised cattle and grew wheat and silage. He was divorced from his wife, but they were still close. Their teenage son, Jim had finished high school and was enrolled at Polytechnic Institute in Billings, now Rocky Mountain College.

Hollowell's ranch was large enough that he had to employ a couple of ranch hands, and someone to maintain the house, but during harvest season he had to hire a large crew of harvesters, mule skinners, drivers, as well as cooks and helpers to feed his harvest crew bringing in the fodder. After an early morning breakfast, the crew would go out into the fields. Around one in the afternoon, suppertime was called, and the men sat down at a large outdoor table near the ranch house and feasted on a huge spread. They relaxed a bit after supper and then went back out into the fields until it got dark. Ranches were rated by harvesters by how good the food was. A good cook was incentive bring in good workers.

For the 1925 harvest season, Hollowell hired a local woman, thirty-five-year old Emma Kerckel as head cook. Emma's husband Gustav Kerckel had abandoned her and their nine children in nearby Fronberg, Montana, leaving the Danish born woman to fend for her family. Emma brought along her seventeen-year old daughter Emma to work as her assistant.

It must have been like heaven sent Hollowell an angel and the two became lovebirds, despite the twenty-five-year age difference. He was a good catch for young Emma, a handsome and successful divorced rancher to rescue her from a life of poverty. Hollowell avowed his love for her in front of many witnesses over the next six months.

Everyone in Carbon County knew that Emma and Hollowell was an item. This seemed to suit the elder Emma fine, she had one less mouth to feed, and beside she had taken up with Samuel Gee, a twenty-four-year-old man from Cody, Wyoming. To keep up resemblance of decorum, young Emma rented a room in Fronberg from family friend Jake Lowe, but she virtually lived at the Hollowell ranch.

On the afternoon of March 25, 1926, Hollowell and his elderly ranch hand Anthony Sancomb came barreling into the town of Bridger in Hollowell's automobile. Screeching to a halt in front of Dr. J.E. Midgett's office, Hollowell ran into the office for the doctor. Doc Midgett came to the car and found young Emma Kerckel quite dead. Sheriff Roberts was called, and he instructed Hollowell and Sancomb to drive up the road to Red Lodge where they would eventually meet up.

Doctor Midgett and undertaker Mrs. H.E. Wolfe took the teenager's body to Wolfe's funeral home for examination. They quickly concluded that Emma had been killed by a blast from a shotgun. She had multiple wounds to her face and neck. Midgett and Wolfe knew there was more to the story than Hollowell was letting on. The shotgun pellets had hit her under the right eye, the right side of her jaw, her right collarbone, and on the left side of her face.

Hollowell and Sancomb started driving to Red Lodge, but abruptly drove back to the ranch. Sancomb told him that the sheriff instructed them to drive directly to Red Lodge, but Hollowell quickly shut him up telling him that he wanted to grab the pistol that Kerckel had dropped. At the ranch Hollowell went into the house, quickly came back out with a pistol and returned to the road to meet the sheriff.

At the Carbon County jail, Hollowell claimed that young Emma came to the ranch while he was working on a mower. He asserted she demanded money owed to her mother from work that she had not been paid for. When Hollowell told her that he did not own her mother any money, young Emma pulled out a pistol and marched the eighty-two-year old Sancomb and Hollowell to the ranch house.

Once inside the house, Hollowell grabbed a shotgun from a closet and pointed it at Emma, who stood in the open doorway. Meaning to shoot the pistol out of Emma's hand, he fired and accidently hit her with buckshot.

The authorities had a few issues with Hollowell's story. It was well known around Bridger that Hollowell and young Emma were having a romantic relationship and that the seventeen-year old often stayed overnight at the ranch. They also found it peculiar that an experienced rancher like Hollowell would not know that a shotgun could not knock a pistol out of her hand, since a shotgun fires pellets in an expanding pattern, and not a solid bullet. They also had problems with Hollowell's story that Emma was over to collect money for her mother. The elder Emma Kerckel took care of her own business and would never send her daughter to do something that she could do herself.

The police, along with the county coroner, Dr. Midgett and the undertaker Mrs. Wolfe went back to the ranch to investigate the crime scene. Deputy F.T. McCall looked around for the mower that Hollowell claimed to be working on when young Emma approached him, and found the area overgrown with vegetation as if it had not been touched since last autumn.

When Anthony Sancomb was questioned, he was not very talkative. He first told the sheriff that he was inside the house and did not see a thing. The law of the west was firmly planted in his soul, the more left unsaid, especially to the law, the better. He was losing his eyesight and his hearing. He had seen so many changes during his long life, he was not sure of anything. One thing he was sure about was the young Emma had stayed overnight many times, including the night before the shooting. He believed that she intended to stay that night too. With careful prodding by Mrs. Wolfe, Sancomb told her that he saw Hollowell walk out of the house with a shotgun raised and aimed at unarmed Emma, who said not a word, and shot her down in cold blood.

The trial started on May 27, 1926 in Red Lodge with Judge Robert Strong presiding. Representing the State of Montana was Carbon County Attorney Emily Sloan, who was the first female to be elected county attorney in Montana and aided by Special Prosecutor C.C. Rowan. Representing Hollowell were attorneys John Skinner and R.G. Wiggenhorn.

To ensure the dignity of the deceased, Judge Strong disallowed any reference to the romantic relationship between Emma and the rancher, as it had already been clarified that the two knew each other. This put a crimp in the prosecutor's argument as Mrs. Sloan and Mr. Rowan had many witnesses who could verify the relationship. They included mother Emma, who in the interim between her daughter's murder and the trial had gotten her divorce and married Samuel Gee.

Hotel clerks Florence Hill of the Lincoln Hotel and Anna France of the Hunter Hot Springs Resort were not allowed to testify about the multiple visits that the couple had made to their hotels. Jack Lowe, Emma's landlord was also forbidden to testify about the couple romantic relationship. Brother and sister Andrew and Maude Langstaff were not allowed to tell the court about giving Emma a ride in their car to the Hollowell Ranch on the day of the murder, but they were not allowed to discuss what they knew about the pair's amorous relationship.

Throughout the trial there was no physical description of Emma. She apparently was a strong and healthy young woman who enjoyed taking horses out for a spirited run. One store clerk described her attire the last time he saw her as wearing a sweater, khaki riding breeches and top riding boots. There was no mention of her Scandinavian heritage, height, hair color, or complexion.

Neither side wanted the elderly Anthony Sancomb on the stand. He had lived in the West since 1876, the year a combined force of Native Americans

25

slaughtered George Custer's Seventh Calvary. He was a man of the west, he did not ask questions, and expected no questions of him.

Sancombs was not fond of the law, and during the original police interview took great offense over Sheriff Roberts suggestion that they take a drive to Red Lodge to talk. Sancombs thought the sheriff was threatening to lock him in jail to beat a witness statement out of him. He may have been right, but the sheriff later explained that he only thought that the old cowboy was embarrassed to talk about the relationship between Kerckel and Hallowell in front of Mrs. Wolfe and would be more comfortable elsewhere. Sancomb's disposition was that of a man who had lived most of his life outside, and alone. The man who was a walking and talking living history book, was kicked to the side, his word was no longer necessary as Mrs. Wolfe, Deputy McCall, Sheriff Roberts and Doc Midgett told the court what Sancomb had mumbled to them back at the ranch during the second investigation.

Sheriff Roberts did ballistic tests on the shotgun and the pistol that Hollowell claimed was held by Emma. The spread from the shotgun showed that for the pattern that hit Emma in the face and neck had to been fired from twenty feet away. The pistol that Emma allegedly had pointed at Hollowell caused a lot of confusion. Jake Lowe was shown the pistol and asked if it was his gun which had gone missing the day of the murder. Lowe was not sure. In the end, the pistol was of no real importance to the case, as Hollowell had admitted to shooting Emma.

The defense was no doubt delighted at the judge's decree that the sexual relationship between the dead teen and the middle-aged rancher could not be brought up at trial. Everyone believed the relationship was the reason for the murder. Hollowell had obviously grown tired of the young woman, and Emma, being of sturdy immigrant stock would not have it. So Hollowell gunned her down as if she were a cow with Hoof and Mouth Disease.

Hollowell took the witness stand and told an unbelievable story, a story that he had two months to dream up. Hollowell told the court that he was working on a mower when Emma suddenly appeared. He said he asked her, "What in hell are

26

you doing there?" Emma responded by asking if his son Jim was home. The question annoyed Hollowell as she knew that he had taken Jim to the Polytechnic Institute in Billings to start college the day before. Then she asked if Sancomb was at the ranch as she was there to borrow his banjo. Angry with Hollowell's aloofness, Emma accused him of spreading rumors about her sexuality. That's when he noticed she had a gun and ordered both men to go into the house. After entering the house, Hollowell grabbed a gun in a closet and faced her.

Standing in the doorway, holding open the screen door, gun in her right and pointed at Hollowell. For at least 10 minutes he pleaded with her to put the gun down. They agreed to put their guns down together. She slumped in the doorway, then straightened up, swung the gun into the air and fired, while saying, "Maybe you think the gun ain't loaded? I came out there to kill you. I am going to shoot you." Hollowell said it was then that he shot her with his shotgun.

The jury, which consisted of ranchers, farmers, and miners, did not believe a word of Hollowell testimony, and quickly found him guilty of Second-Degree Murder. He was sentenced to ten to twenty years in prison.

A Guy Who Never Got a Break

March 29, 1926
South Bend, Indiana
Murderer – John Hall
Victim – Louis Kriedler

It was supposed to be an easy robbery for John Hall and Tom O'Brien. Go into the drug store, rob the register, and leave. They were not expecting anyone to put up a fight, but as the robbery was in progress, owner and druggist Louis Kriedler entered his store. Kriedler had just come from the bank, and under his arm was envelope with over three-thousand dollars inside it. Kriedler pulled out his revolver and pulled the trigger. To everyone's amazement, the gun failed to fire. The twenty-one-year-old Hall grabbed the gun away from Kriedler and pistol-whipped him. Kriedler crumpled onto the floor as the two men made their getaway. Kriedler suffered from his injury until he died on April 5, 1926.

Not exactly geniuses, Hall and O'Brien, stayed in northern Indiana and were caught by Elkhart police on May 10, 1926. Confinement did not suit the pair, and together they planned to escape. Their first attempt failed, but on September 16, 1926, the pair sawed through the bars on their cell and escaped. Hall was apprehended almost immediately, but O'Brien made good his escape.

At the trial Hall was brought into the courtroom in handcuffed and shackles. He sat surrounded by officers, including one standing behind him cradling a shotgun. The D.A. immediately told the court that Hall's real name was Grazyb, and he was from Milwaukee, where his mother still resided. The trial was quick, and he was found guilty of first-degree murder and robbery on October 6, 1926. John Grazyb was sentenced to the electric chair at the Indiana State Prison in Michigan City on January 21, 1927.

Thomas O'Brien was nabbed by police in Chicago, tried for the robbery/murder and was sentenced to life in prison on May 5, 1927. Grazyb felt that he got a raw deal and desperately filed appeals. Indiana Governor Edward L. Jackson gave

Grazyb two reprieves, but then agreed that the judge and jury had done the right thing. Through his attorney, O'Brien petitioned the Governor to change Grazyb's sentence to life. He stated that it was he who had hit Kriedler with his gun, leading to his death. O'Brien knew that since he was already convicted of the crime, they could not resentence him. Governor Jackson did not buy it, and ordered that Hall be executed on April 10, 1928. Hall was resigned to his fate, telling reporters, "I'm just one of the guys who never got a break"

On his final day, Hall had a chicken dinner, smoked a corncob pipe and chatted with his guards. No family members came to visit. He left his cell at 12:01a.m., and one minute later the first jolt of electricity boiled his blood. He died seven minutes later. He was the thirteen prisoner to die in Indiana's electric chair.

That day, the Hammond- Lake County newspaper ran headlines that read "John Hall Who "Never Got a Break" Dies Today in the Electric Chair."

By May 6, 1928, no one from Grazyb's family came forward to claim his body and he was buried in the prison cemetery.

Dummkopf

May 1, 1926

Beim – Roosevelt County, Montana

Murderer – Ferdinand Schlaps

Victims – Anton Geisler / Lumilla Geisler

Martin and Christiana Schlaps were illiterate immigrant farmers from German speaking Russia. Eking out a living outside of Ashely, North Dakota was tough, but having eleven children made it easier. German was the language spoken in rural North Dakota in 1926. English was only spoken by schoolteachers and cops. They lived a lot like they had in the German colonies in what now is Romania. The families were huge, because there was always a couple of children who died in childbirth or did not make to adulthood.

Their children, Jacob, Martin, Mary, John, Rebecka, Ferdinand, Andrew, Hulda, Theodore, Albert, and David were needed on the farm during growing season. There were no games of baseball played by the boys. The males in the family only knew toil and work. The Schlaps boys were driving teams of heavy horses plowing the flat fields by the time they were ten years old, and if they lived to fourteen, they were sent off to work at neighboring farms, with Martin and Christiana keeping all the money they earned. This was expected of their sons until they turned twenty-one. The females would be married off before they were eighteen, sometimes to men who they had not met before their wedding day. One of their daughters had already married and moved four-hundred miles northwest to Homestead, Montana, where her husband, Jack Wolf leased a spread known as the McNeil farm.

Ferdinand, known as Fred to his family, was the fifth of eight brothers in the Schlaps family. At sixteen with the equivalent of a fourth-grade education he was turned out to a neighboring farm to earn money for his parents. The Schlaps' children were basically indentured servants who milked cows, threshed wheat and plowed the soil from sunrise to sundown. Certainly, there was talk among the

30

brothers about how unfair it was that they worked like animals only to have their parents keep their earnings. They knew in America they could break the old traditions. They dreamt of a better and more meaningful life than their parents lived. That was not to be.

Fred was kicked in the head by a horse in 1925 and was unconscious for twelve hours. It took him six weeks before he got his strength back. During this time his father began selling off the family farm, fields and machinery. Whatever the tightlipped Schlaps were planning they did not publicize their plans. It could have been possible that Martin, flush with dollars wanted to return to the old country. It could be possible that Martin wanted to move farther west and continue to rent out his sons for hard labor to needy wheat farmers in Northern Montana. It did not matter because by the time Fred stopped hearing little birds tweeting in his head, old Martin had mysteriously died.

By the spring of 1926, fifty-one-year-old Christiana and at least three of the boys, including Fred, moved to her daughter's farm in Roosevelt County, Montana. Before Fred had a chance to unpack, Christiana rented him to neighboring farm as a hired hand. As habit, his paycheck went directly to her.

Alton and Lumilla Geisler had lived on their farmstead for several years and were well-liked in the community. Thirty-nine-year old Alton, who was called Tony, was an educated man who knew a lot about running a successful farm. Lumilla was a tall, attractive thirty-one-year old. They were a good looking, hard-working couple who ran a modern farm about twenty miles west of the McNeil place. Fred had a bunk in the barn, and ate with the couple, but was uncommunicative and socially awkward.

Fred did not like his employers. He felt they worked him too hard and treated him badly. In many ways, Fred was no smarter than a cow chewing cud. He did not know how to act around strangers and lacked logical ability. Fred creeped out the Geisler's and they kept their distance from him.

The couple had every reason to want to keep the lurking idiot at arm's length, because Fred planned on murdering them shortly after he was hired. Fred wanted

31

Geisler's shiny new Ford sedan. In his unsophisticated brain, he assumed that he would have it made in life, if he had that car back in Ashely, North Dakota.

Everyone who lived between the Geisler farm and the McNeil ranch thought it was peculiar to see Fred speeding down the dirt road in Geisler's new Ford. The Geisler's were not the type of people who would allow their dim-witted eighteen-year-old farmhand to drive off in their new car.

May 2, 1926 was a Sunday. A man who operated an irrigation gate on the Big Muddy River, outside of Homestead, Montana, noticed the nearly naked body of Lumilla Geisler floating in the canal. A large gaping hole in her neck was visible, as well as one in her groin. A little farther down the channel was Tony's bloated body with a big hole in his shoulder.

Sheridan County Sheriffs discovered dried blood on the guardrail of the bridge over the canal and drag marks alongside to near where the bodies were found. Some recognized the bodies as the young couple with the farm over near Beim in Roosevelt County. It appeared that the couple were murdered in Roosevelt County and disposed twenty miles away. A call went out to Sheriff Rodney Salisbury in Wolf Point.

The sheriff, along with several deputized citizens drove over the McNeil Ranch where they were sure that Fred Schlaps and the Geisler car would be. When they drove into the farmyard of the McNeil Ranch, they saw the Schlaps boys and Jack Wolf admiring the Ford. Sheriff Salisbury politely greeted the young men and started questioning Fred while he inspected the car. He noticed blood on the running board. When the sheriff questions Fred about the blood, the young man broke down and confessed, much to the shock of his family.

After walking the Sheriff and his men through the murder scene and showing them the route to where he unceremoniously dumped the bodies, Fred sat down in the prosecutor's office and wrote down his confession.

Tony and I were in the barn putting the harnesses on the horses, and I told Tony I was going to the house to get a drink of water, and at the same time I planned that I would get the twelve-gauge shotgun and some shells in the house *and come back to the barn where Tony was. When I was getting the shells and gun in the house, Mrs. Geisler asked me what I wanted with the gun and the shells, and I told her I was going hunting. Then I went to the barn and found that Tony was outside the barn. I kept kind of hidden until I got near the barn door on the east side of the barn. Tony was standing there looking east from the barn. I took aim at his left shoulder on the side on which his heart is and fired. He fell to the ground and tried to get up again. I put another shell into the gun and fired at his head the second time, and he did not move any more after that. I then loaded the gun again and went up to the house where Mrs. Geisler was. I walked up near the window the south side of the house and saw Mrs. Geisler standing in the bedroom looking north. I put the gun up and shot Mrs. Geisler. She hollered, but I could not understand what she said. Then I loaded the gun and went into the bedroom where she had been, and she was not there. Then I came back out into the room where I slept, and she was hid [sic] behind the clothes curtain. The first shot struck her on the left arm and side. Then I aimed at her again and fired; the second shot struck her in the neck, cutting away about one-third of her neck. Tony did not see me before I shot him; neither did Mrs. Geisler the first time. After both of them were dead, then I picked up the empty shells, put the gun away, and then threw the empty shells away in the creek bottom. Then I got a pail of water and the mop and washed up all around the house where there was blood. There was blood all around the bedroom where Mrs. Geisler was standing the first time, I shot her. After I got everything all cleaned up, then I covered the oats in the wagon with a blanket to keep the horses and cattle from eating them. Then I went and unharnessed the horses and turned them loose. The first thing I done after cleaning up the blood in the house was to look for money. I found about $20 in the trunk; a $10 paper bill and some silver. It was in a pocketbook, and I put them all in my pocket. The night before I saw the pocketbook in the trunk because the trunk was open. Then I gave the cattle water. Then I got the car out and filled it up with* *gasoline. Then I stayed around the place until it commenced to get dark. Then I loaded the two bodies into the Ford sedan. Then I drove the car with the bodies into the Big Muddy toward Homestead. When I got on the bridge, I threw Mrs. Geisler's body into the river. Then I saw a car coming, so I drove up to the right along the river. I put the lights out on the car and waited until the car went by. Then I put Tony's body into the Big Muddy. Then I went to Homestead and stayed there about an hour and a half. Then I drove to my mother's place. The next morning, early, I washed the blood out of the Ford car. Then in the afternoon the sheriff and county attorney from Plentywood came over to the place where I was at my mother's place. They asked me about it, and I told them that I had taken Tony and his wife to Poplar; they were going to a hospital. There was some blood on my clothes, and they asked me about the blood on my clothes and the Ford car, and I finally told them that I had done it. Then I went with the said officers to the Tony Geisler place and showed them just how I had killed Tony Geisler and his wife. That I had planned on going to North Dakota that evening with the car and go to Ashley.*

The caskets containing the Geisler's were shipped to Shiner, Texas where they were buried. A trial was held during the third week of July in Wolf Point. It was an open and shut case, with a signed confession. In hopes that Schlaps would escape the death penalty, the defense laid on thick the defendant's lack of education, his difficulties with the English language and American culture. The story of his harsh upbringing did not cause any sympathy among harden, saddle-sore ranchers who served on the jury. They had lived hard lives and they never killed anyone because of it.

On July 24, 1926, Ferdinand Schlaps was found guilty of the murder of Lumilla Geisler. On August 8, he was sentenced to be hanged at the Wolf Point jail. After the usual dog and pony show at the court of appeals, Schlaps time was up. At midnight on a stormy May 20, 1927, Schlaps was led through the jail yard of the Roosevelt County Jail and up the recently constructed gallows. The trapdoors opened at 12:10 and Schlaps body swayed and spun slowly in the pouring rain until he was declared dead at 12:22am. His family claimed his body.

Michigan Mail Bomb

May 27, 1926

Blue Lake Township, Michigan

Murderer – Asa Bartlett

Victims – August Krubaech / Jeanette Krubaech / William Frank

Blue Lake Township, Michigan sits ten miles, as the crow flies from the coast of Lake Michigan. It is surrounded by the 540,322-acre Manistee National Forest, ensuring that future generations will enjoy the thousands of lakes, ponds, rivers and wildlife.

It was a beautiful May morning at the Three Lakes Tavern. The owner, August Krubaech, known to his friends as Gus, was going through his mail. There was more mail than usual because his daughter Jeanette was getting married in two days, and gifts and cards were arriving from far and near.

Nineteen-year old Jeanette and her twenty-two-year old fiancé William Frank were on their way to nearby Muskegon to get their marriage license, but with so much mail for them they thought it would be fun to go through it first. The couple clambered up to the bar where August was sorting his bills, personal letters, and junk mail from the wedding cards and gifts.

Mrs. Krubaech was within earshot of her daughter as she went about cleaning up and restocking the tavern. Local man, Thornton Russell stopped in, and cigar-maker Louis Kolb arrived with a new stock of cigars for the bar. Bridesmaid Myrtle Whittier, nee Krubaech, was flitting around the inn. It was a busier morning than usual and was about to get busier.

The Krubaech's had moved from Chicago to Blue Lake Township in 1913 when he and his wife established the tavern/resort a stone's throw from idyllic Big Blue Lake. The Krubaech's and their tavern were popular with the locals, and business was good.

Gus was a civic minded man who had run for the position of Blue Lake Township Supervisor several times. He had lost to Jennie Norlin by one vote in

1922 but won in 1926 in a landslide. Norlin received only twenty-one votes. Norlin was the handpicked candidate of the Muskegon chapter of the Ku Klux Klan, and her defeat angered the local KKK.

By 1926, the Ku Klux Klan, which became very powerful in the early part of the 1920's partially because of their pro-prohibition, pro-Protestant, pro-Caucasian, anti-immigrant, and anti-Catholic position was being abandoned by most of their members. A murder/sex scandal involving the Indiana delegation had soured the members, many who saw it as a club like the Kiwanis or Lion's Club. Hating immigrants, Jews. Catholics and African Americans is one thing, but murder and rape was not what they signed up for.

Nobody in Blue Lake Township was more irritated by Krubaech's win than World War I veteran, and Blue Lake Township constable, Asa Bartlett. The twenty-eight-year-old blacksmith also supplemented his income as a stump blaster. In 1926, the entire state of Michigan was a sea of tree stumps. The virgin White Pine was clear-cut by the lumber barons and by the 1880's most of northern Michigan was reduced to flammable brush and stumps. To clear the land for farming, the stumps had to be removed, and that was done with dynamite. Bartlett was handy with tools and dynamite. He was also suspected of being the Exalted Cyclops of the Muskegon County branch of the KKK.

Among the pile of mail, August found a package, and thinking that it was a wedding gift, he slid it over to Jeanette and William to open. Suddenly a blast ripped half of the two-story tavern apart. When the dust cleared, William Frank was dead. August had his right arm blown off and had a deep gash in his torso. The blast, which was heard two miles away, blew Jeanette's eyes out of their sockets and left her a bloody and moaning mess. Russell was knocked off his feet and pinned against a wall by a heavy slot machine. Kolb was knocked down, but otherwise okay. Luckily, Mrs. Krubaech and her daughter Myrtle were out of the room when the bomb went off and were unharmed.

Gus died in the hospital two-hours later. Jeanette survived until the next morning. Her dying words were "Opie." her pet name for her fiancé. Instead of a wedding, the family was having a triple funeral.

It did not take long for Muskegon County Sheriff Lyman Covell, along with bomb experts from the Michigan State Police and the federal government to determine the culprit. A search of Bartlett's property found an old rifle with the trigger mechanism missing. Doctors had found a trigger and spring imbedded in Gus Krubaech's body. It was a perfect match.

Pieces of the package that held the booby-trap bomb survived, including the pre-paid parcel stamp that was purchased in nearby Montague three days before. The post office clerks remembered Bartlett purchasing it and the numbers of the transaction matched. The bomb was mailed from Muskegon on May 26, where Bartlett was seen by many witnesses. Add Bartlett's access to dynamite, his tool making skills and his expressed hatred of Krubaech, it did not take much to convince Bartlett to plead guilty. Bartlett allegedly told the police, "I could not stand to have Krubaech running the township, [but] I am certainly sorry about killing Jeanette and Franke. I did not think about the wedding when I sent the bomb."

Bartlett was sentence to "life," and probably because he was a peace officer, he was spared the bleak walls of the state prison in Jackson and was shipped off to the state prison in Marquette, two hundred and thirty miles north of Muskegon.

After thirty-six years as a model prisoner, Asa Bartlett had his sentenced reduced to "time served," by then governor George Romney in 1963. He went to live with a cousin in Oceana County and worked as a handyman. He died in 1982 at the age of eighty-five in a medical care facility.

Jeanette Krubaech would have been seventy-four had Bartlett not murdered her.

So, My Toddler is an Axe Murderer

May 30, 1926
Provo, Utah
Murderer – James Earl Brand
Victim – William Brand

Four-year old James Brand was playing with his three-year old brother in the backyard of their grandmother's home in Provo, Utah. It was a beautiful Sunday afternoon. Out of the blue, James picked up a dull hatchet that was laying around in the yard and struck his little brother over the head. The tyke struck the toddler in the head over a dozen times before an adult intervened. Little William died a few hours later in the hospital.

James was the first-born child of James and Grace Brand, a young Mormon couple starting a family together. James told the police that a few months before, some neighbors caught the little boy doing some frivolous mischief, and to frighten him told him that they were going to chop off his head.

They dragged the screaming boy over to a handy chopping block and forced him to lay his head on it. Ever since then the boy suffered from nightmares and started acting violent towards his playmates. A few weeks earlier, he had killed a cat with a garden hoe.

James was brought to a psychiatric hospital for observation and released to his parents the next day. Hopefully they were instructed to hide all sharp instruments from him.

Popular columnist Arthur Brisbane wrote a little tidbit about the tragedy and erroneously wrote the father was the person who cruelly dragged little James to the chopping block. The story was repeated in Hearse Newspapers across the nation. Arthur eventually went insane.

James Brand died on March 29, 1929 of epilepsy at the age of seven.

Incest in Seattle

June 16, 1926
Seattle, Washington
Murderer - Wallace Gaines
Victim – Sara Gaines

People love their children, but before the twentieth century most people had children, so they would have another field-hand or milkmaid. People had a lot of children too and not only because there was no such thing as birth control, but the chances of a child reaching adulthood was not that great. Children were expendable. A simple scratch could become infected, and you would die. A simple medical procedure now, was a death sentence in those days before antibiotics. Childbirth was dangerous too, as complication could easily kill the mother. With mom dead the family structure would often fall apart, with children being sent to live with relatives, or to orphanages. Children could be traded off to farmers or tradesmen to work off the parent's debt. Some children joined circuses or went to sea. Others just lived on the streets, committing crimes or prostituting themselves.

World War I and the Spanish Flu Pandemic put such a big crimp in the population that many survivors acquired a new outlook on raising children. Death puts an entirely new meaning to life, and when deaths are counted by the tens of millions, it can tip the balance of sanely loving your child. Wallace Cloyes Gaines was a World War I veteran who went too far.

Wallace Cloyes Gaines was probably born in 1880, in Framingham, Massachusetts, not exactly a great era to have entered the world, but we don't really get a choice. He married South Lynnfield, Massachusetts resident Sylvia Howard around 1902.

In 1904, their daughter Silvia was born and by 1909, Wallace, who was known as Bob, had left the family and headed to Seattle, where his brother William lived. The couple divorced not long after.

40

The world went to war in 1914, but the United States held back joining the disaster until 1917. The Selective Service started drafting men, at first twenty-one to thirty-year old's, but as the soldiers were being slaughtered on the fields of France, men eighteen to forty-five-years old were conscripted into service.

Bob would have been thirty-seven-years old when he entered the Army. He was assigned to the 41st Division, 161st Infantry and saw heavy action in France. There is no record of what exactly befell Bob on those killing fields, whether he was injured, gassed or just seen too many of his comrades senselessly slaughtered. Bob was given full disability benefits and discharged.

Bob was a heavy drinker before the war and became a heavier drinker after it. With prohibition in full sail when Bob came back to Seattle, moonshine, rotgut and grain alcohol was the order of the day. After ten years of bachelorhood, Bob tied the knot with a skinny, fragile woman named Elizabeth. They lived in a one-bedroom home at 108 - N 51st Street, in Seattle's Green Lake neighborhood. Bob collected disability money from his Army wounds and worked sporadically as a mining engineer. His brother William was the Chairman of the King County Commissioners and it was hinted that he threw Bob work assignments.

King County encompasses over two thousand square miles, or roughly twice the size of the state of Rhode Island. The county varies in terrain from the bubonic tidal flats of Vashon Island to the jagged, glacier covered peaks of the Cascade Mountains. Rich in natural resources and blessed with the natural deep-water port of Seattle, the commissioners wield great provincial power.

In the fall of 1925, Bob's daughter Silvia, a 1925 graduate of prestigious Smith College, came to Seattle to be with her father. They had not seen each other in sixteen years. The trio shared the little one-bedroom house, with Sylvia sleeping on the couch, but after a couple of weeks, Elizabeth ended up on the couch. Sylvia and Bob loved each other so much, that they blatantly broke the universal taboo, incest.

At first the situation bothered Elizabeth enough that she shot herself in the head on Thanksgiving, 1925. She only got a flesh wound and was stitched up by

41

the family doctor. Neighbors raised their eyebrows as the trio loudly and regularly argued their problems out.

Uncle William got his niece a job with the King County Title Trust Company and with that came more independence. She was working in downtown Seattle but was not enjoying the nightlife with people her own age. Instead she was drinking rotgut booze and having a torrid sexual relationship with her forty-six-year-old father, and possibly, her stepmother.

It would be crass to say that all good things must come to an end, but by the summer of 1926, Sylvia was fed up with the drinking, the sex and her drunken father. She went to Uncle William and asked him to help her find other lodgings.

On evening of June 16, 1926, the couple argued publicly at a drug store, resulting in Sylvia storming off by herself. Bob made a comment about "women and their emotions" to the pharmacist, who brushed off the matter. That was the last time Sylvia Gaines was seen alive.

The next morning two carpenters, J.L. Reynolds and O.B. Ripley were on their way to work when they noticed a pair of women's slippers along the northeast shore of Green Lake between Orin Court North and Meridian Avenue North. Their curiosity got the best of them, so they followed into the bulrushes, where the found the battered and nearly nude body of Sylvia Gaines.

The police found a ghastly crime scene. It appeared that Sylvia was surprised right out of her slippers. She ran into a stream that ran along the lake where she was tackled and beaten to death with a blunt object. Her clothing was in shreds, and she appeared to have been posed in an obscene position, making authorities believe that she had been sexually assaulted.

Bob reported his daughter missing about the same time as the police arrived at the crime scene. Sylvia was identified by her father. The public was in an uproar. There was a similar murder in which a young woman was found murdered elsewhere in King County and it was at first believed that the two murders were connected. Seattle had its share of murders, but they were usually drunken sailors or transients, not beautiful, young, educated women from the East Coast with a relative who was elected to one of the most powerful positions in the state. The case became a top priority for the Seattle Police Department.

The funeral for Sylvia Gaines was held on July 10. Her Uncle William wept throughout the service. Bob was stoic. She was cremated, and her ashes were sent to her mother in Massachusetts.

The police were suspicious of Wallace Gaines. The detectives noted that Gaines was under the influence of alcohol every time that met with him. His friends and neighbors were very candid to the police about what was going on in the little house. Things like this did not happen in the sleepy city, populated with working class, first and second-generation Scandinavian Lutherans.

After Wallace Gaines was hauled down to police headquarters for his fourth interview, his brother William told the press, "My brother is being crucified, I tell you. He is innocent, innocent as a new-born babe. They have grilled him cruelly four times and still he is not under arrest."

Despite the Chairman of the King County Commissioners protests, the police arrested Bob and charged him with murder.

The trial started on August 2, 1926, and prosecutor Ewing Colvin pulled out all the stops. He summarized Gaines life, from his east coast upbringing, his failed marriage to Sylvia's mother, his abandonment of his wife and child that led to his divorce. He spotlighted his drinking habits before and after his service in the U.S. Army and the "unnatural" relationship that he had with his long-lost daughter. One by one, witnesses were brought onto the stand and told their stories.

Neighbor Deeta McAuliffe testified that Gaines had told him before the murder that, "if Sylvia goes back to Boston, I am going to bunch her." When McAuliffe asked what Bob meant, he replied, "If she goes, I won't be far back of her."

The pharmacist told his story about the spat that happened between father and daughter on the night of the murder. He stated that Bob was so angry that he pulled Sylvia out of his 1918 Buick Roadster, by the collar of her coat, after which she stormed off down the sidewalk with Bob chasing after her.

43

Gaines' mechanic Harry Wurster testified that he saw Gaines' distinctive roadster parked by the murder scene, at around the time of the crime .Another neighbor, Olive Memmer, told the court that she had overheard Sylvia tell her uncle William she wanted to move out of her father's home because "I can't stand it any longer. I'm tired of four walls and moonshine bottles."

Dr. Dudley Long testified about how he treated Mrs. Gaines for the slight gunshot wound that she inflicted on Thanksgiving. He noticed something odd about Bob and Sylvia's behavior.

A Seattle police officer testified that he had been patrolling a lover's lane near Woodland Park, which abuts Green Lake, and discovered Bob and Sylvia necking in the roadster. He told the court that as he approached the car, he could see the couple fumble with their clothing. There was a problem with the vehicle's registration, and they were told to follow him to the Wallingford Precinct station, where the matter was straightened out.

Even Bob's best friend Louis Sterns, testified against him. The two friends lived only a few miles away from each other and regularly drank alcohol together. He told the court that Bob was expected at his house at 4217-2nd Avenue NW on evening of June 16th, but he showed up late, disheveled and drunk.

Sterns told the court what Gaines had conveyed to him that evening.

"You know what I have always told you, that if anyone in my house told me when I should come and go and when I should drink and how much, I would kill em? Well, that's what happened."

A maid from the Artic Hotel in downtown Seattle testified that she had accidently walked in on the couple in their hotel room on Thanksgiving Day. They were in bed together and in their nightclothes. Bob covered his face with a sheet.

The prosecution had more up their sleeves, including blood stains that matched Sylvia's on his clothing. But the kicker for the forensic case against Gaines was the murder weapon. Police had dragged Green Lake looking for a murder weapon. They found the crank starter wrench for a 1918 Buick Roadster.

Checking with neighbors if Gaines used a crank starter for his car, they all said yes. Examining Gaines roadster, they discovered that its crank was missing.

The jury was out for three hours and the verdict was guilty and sentenced to death. Gaines fainted when he heard the decree. He was taken to the Washington State Penitentiary in Walla Walla and housed on Death Row.

With his appeals gone, and the governor unwilling to pardon Gaines, he wrote the following letter to his family in Framingham, Massachusetts on the day before he was executed.

This may be my farewell letter to you. It is seven forty a.m. and I haven't heard a thing from the Governor and don't know if he is going to do anything or not. Things don't look any too good and I am prepared for the worst. If they kill me tomorrow, Colvin and a few others are responsible for my murder. I am prepared to meet my Maker, whatever happens. I wish to thank you and your husband from the bottom of my heart for all you have done for me. If I pass out, my wife is going to New York to live and you will see her. Please be good to her as she is a precious jewel if ever there was one and has been a real comfort to me in all my trouble and misery. Bill is taking this thing harder than any of us. I'm all right and have made my peace with God. Two Catholic priests were up to see me yesterday and I still had to have my little joke. One of them asked me when I wanted to see him again and I told him, Saturday. Well there isn't much more that I can write to your except that when I meet my Creator face to face, I won't have to answer to a murder charge, and he is the supreme judge and ruler overall. Once more I say goodbye, and may God love and protect you and your family.

On August 31, 1928, a noose was put around the forty-eight-year-old neck of Wallace Gaines, and he dropped through the trap to his death. He was buried with military honors by the American Legion.

A grove of Alders was planted as a memorial to Sylvia Gaines near the murder site. The area is known as Gaines Point.

Urge For Overkill

June 28, 1926 / May 26, 1927

Tampa, Florida

Murderer – Benjamin Franklin Levins

Victims – Bee Rowell / Caroline Rowell / Eva Rowell / Charles H. Alexander
Herman Merrill / Nettie Merrill / Merrell Merrill / Ralph Merrill / Mildred Merrill
S.J. Ellis / Hugh Edward McRae / B.M. Davidson / Hal Pifer / Earl McGill

Ruby Silner did not know what she was getting into the morning she walked up to the Rowell home on June 28, 1926. Ruby was going job hunting with her friend, sixteen-year old Eva Lena Rowell, who lived at the large home with her extended family. Silner, along with her father, who was going to drive the pair around Tampa for their appointments, were perplexed when their knock at the normally crowded house was not answered. Looking through a window, they saw a bloody body lying on the parlor floor. They yelled for the police.

The police went through the house, room by room, finding four dead, their heads bashed to a pulp. In a back room they found Eva Rowell, her face battered and barely alive. The gore-covered murder weapon was found lying on the floor next to Eva's bed. She was taken to a hospital where she died a few hours later without regaining consciences. In addition to Eva, her forty-five- year old uncle Bee Rowell, her elderly grandmother Caroline, and a boarder, thirty-six-year-old Charles Alexander were discovered with their heads and faces chopped up. Missing from the house was Caroline's son, and Eva's father Richard Rowell.

Because of the ferocity of the crime, Police at first suspected Richard and another brother, Henry, who did not live at the home, of the crime. The police sent out an all-points bulletin for the brothers. Tampa only had a population of fifty thousand people in 1926, so the brothers soon found out about tragedy at the home they grew up at and ran to the scene. Their grief made the police look at another set of suspects.

Florida State Police helped the Tampa police with the investigation. The Rowell family had lived in Tampa for decades and was well-known in their neighborhood. Caroline, who owned the house was somewhere between ninety-four and one hundred four years old, nobody knew. Detectives had to shift through generations of neighbors, employers, employees, lodgers, and business associates in hopes of finding a motive for the carnage.

Police picked up Lee Weaver, a young man who had visited Eva at the house on the evening of the murders. They also picked up Bee's drinking buddies, O. F. Fortner, E.S. Keen and W.S. Smith. The three men had also been over to the house on the evening of the murders, drinking with Bee in the kitchen of the home. It was known that Bee, who worked as a carpenter, had recently been robbed of four hundred dollars. He refused to go to the police about the robbery, insisting that he knew who took the money and would take care of the matter himself.

Detectives scrambled around Tampa's Channel District shaking down all their informants, and threatening parolees for information about the thief. No amount of kicks, slaps or punches in those pre-Miranda day could get any of the usual suspects to talk.

The police next tracked down William Johnson and Cappie Carey who caused a ruckus the week before when Bee evicted the unmarried couple from the house. Cappie's husband Elijah Carey was arrested with the pair for good measure. By August all the suspects were released, and the case went cold.

On May 26, 1927, almost a year after the Rowell massacre, eight-year old Hugh Merrill woke up on the floor of his bedroom. He had fallen out of bed during the night, and being a heavy sleepy, did not wake up. Walking into his parent's room, he found them dead. Running from the house, he ran right into his sixteen-year old brother Kenneth, who had slept over at a friend's house that night. They called the police.

Tampa police were stunned to find an almost exact crime scene as the Rowell incident. Forty-three-year-old Herman and his thirty-five-year old wife Nettie were found in their bed with the faces bashed in. In a different room, eleven-year old

Ralph, five-year old Mildred and three-month old baby, Merrell were found with crushed heads. A bloody railroad spike was found at the scene.

Police questioned Hugh, Kenneth and another son, eighteen-year old Gilbert who was working in Orlando if their parents had any enemies. They came up blank. Herman, known as Lonnie, worked as a carpenter in Tampa. Despite having the same occupation and being around the same age as Bee Rowell, the two men did not know each other. The family had only lived in the three-room cottage for a few months. Police found out that the previous tenant was Ed Rowell and his family. Ed was another of Caroline's sons.

There is an old expression, "loose lips sink ships," and in this case too much talk brought attention to two shabbily dressed men, Benjamin Franklin Levins and Leonard Thompson. The pair had spoken to a fortune teller the morning after the Merrill murders and asked if they would be caught.

Later that day, while in a restaurant Levins had read aloud the article about the murders as reported by the newspaper to Thompson. The restaurant owner informed the police, as did the fortune teller. The answer the fortune teller gave the men was never reported.

Levins told the police and prosecutors that he was a fisherman by trade, and a dope fiend for amusement. He admitted to the police he had killed the Merrill family.

When the news hit the streets of Tampa that the axe murderer was caught and had confessed, a lynch mob formed. Every evening from May 30 to June 1, a group of two-thousand angry Floridians threw bricks, taunted and took potshots at the police guarding the jail.

Hillsborough County Sheriff Luther Heirs secretly had his men take Levins to the jail in Orlando for his own safekeeping. He informed the mob that the prisoner had been moved and was safely being guarded at an undisclosed location. The fervent throng did not believe the forty-seven-year old Spanish/American War veteran and continued their attacks. At one point a group wielding a large timber as a battering ram smashed a hole into a jailhouse wall. The waiting police fired a volley of gunfire, injuring eight of the rioters. They were quickly arrested.

The Florida National Guard was called in and they set up machine guns in strategic positions to safeguard the jail. The pinnacle of the attempted lynching occurred when the National Guard opened fire on the rioters after they were shot at from the crowd. Twenty-one rioters were injured by gun fire, and S.J. Ellis, Hugh Edward McRae, B.M. Davidson, Hal Pifer, and Earl McGill were killed. The riot petered out after representatives of the lynch mob were allowed to search the jail for Levins. While in the jail in Orlando, Levins told the assembled detectives, police, guards and prosecutors that he was also responsible for the Rowell massacre almost a year earlier.

The burly fisherman told the astonished group that on June 28, 1926, he had gotten into a confrontation with boarder Charles Alexander over a woman and killed him in the Rowell home. To cover up the crime, he crept through the house and killed everyone he found. The next morning, he signed up on a fishing boat and disappeared on the Gulf of Mexico.

Arriving back to Tampa, almost a year later, he met Thompson and together they drank ethanol, until Thompson passed out near the railroad tracks by the Merrill home. In his ethanol-soaked brain, Levins believed that Frank Rowell lived at the three-room cottage. He crept through an open window and killed everyone with a pointed mallet, not knowing that a different family resided at the house.

Once the trial started, Levins changed his mind and stated that he was coerced by Tampa police while he was being held in Orlando during the riots. Levins testified while he was in Orlando for safe keeping, Tampa police detectives force him to confess to both massacres by threatening to take him back to Tampa to face the lynch mob. Terrified, Levins told the court that he agreed. He also testified that while in police custody he was beaten by a group of unknown men inside the Tampa City Prison.

49

None of Levin's' testimony could help him. He had admitted to killing Lonnie Merrill, and that was the only charge filed against the fisherman. He was found guilty and sentenced to death on July 29, 1927.

Leonard Thompson went on trial on September 6, 1927 for the murder of three-year old Wallace and eleven-year old Ralph Merrill, but the state's star witness, Benjamin Franklin Levins put the trial to a screeching halt. Instead of testifying as he did during his trial that he had killed Lonnie and Nettie, while Thompson murdered the children, Levins told the court that he committed the murders and Thompson had nothing to do with the crime.

Having no alternative, Judge F.M. Robles turned to the defendant and said, "Thompson, you are discharged." Leonard Thompson was a free man.

On November 22, 1927, Benjamin Franklin Levins, a simple Gulf of Mexico fisherman whose jealousy over a woman led to the deaths of fourteen people, sat down in the electric chair at the Florida State Prison in Raiford, Florida and was executed.

Three Bullets for Her Husband

July 2, 1926
San Jose, California
Murderer – Helen Letcher
Victim – Clarence Letcher

Helen Letcher was furious at her husband Clarence. She had hired private detectives to tail him to confirm what she already knew; her husband was having an affair. The twice divorced owner of successful auto repair garage was a San Jose civic booster and leader of the growing city's sporting, business and political circles. Together the couple was the toast of San Jose's social scene and were well known for their parties at their vacation home in the nearby Santa Cruz Mountains.

The private detectives told Helen that her husband was romantically involved with Ann Bennett, a divorcee, who lived at the Hotel Vendome in San Francisco. The same building that Helen's niece, Bonnie Hoff lived. The wealthy couple's marriage had been on shaky ground for at least a year. Clarence had file for divorce in San Francisco earlier in the year but withdrew the petition shortly afterwards.

Clarence told Helen that he was going hunting on the last weekend of June, but Helen was onto him. She called her detective and together they staked out the Hotel Vendome all Saturday and into Sunday. Clarence finally sauntered out of the building on Van Ness on Sunday afternoon and was greeted by Helen. The couple walked off together seemingly to worked things out. However, it was discovered that a few days later, Helen attempted suicide by drinking poison.

On July 2, 1926, the couple was having a heated discussion in front of Letcher's shop, while hundreds of people ambled around them going about their business. Letcher's garage was located at 214 North First Street, right in the middle of downtown San Jose and a stone throw from the Santa Clara County Courthouse. Suddenly, Helen pulled out a revolver and fired four rounds. The first

51

one missed but grazed a passerby. The next two bullets tore into his chest, and the third hit him in the mouth. Helen saved the last bullet for herself, placing the pistol against her temple, and ending her life there and then.

Bonnie Hoff got the news about the murder/suicide and lay in wait for Ann Bennett to come back to her apartment. She accosted Bennett and accused her of instigating the tragedy. Frightened Bennett first fled to a cabin in the Santa Cruz Mountains, before she left for Los Angeles. At first the police wanted to speak to her, but as they discovered that is was a crime of passion, they let her go.

The couple were buried together, however when Clarence's will was found, it was discovered that he wanted to be cremated. He was exhumed, and his ashes spread over the Santa Cruz Mountains via airplane. Helen's body was left in the grave until her family could find her will. Clarence left his only son, George, two-hundred-fifty-thousand dollars.

Panic in Cicero

July 11, 1926
Cicero, Illinois
Murderers – James Crisius / Thomas McWaine
Victims – Marie Blang / Frederick Hein / Ludwig Rose

Twenty-one-year old Chicagoan, James Crisius was angry and wanted revenge. The machinist, who also went by the name James Granite, was fired for losing his left thumb in an industrial accident at the American Flange and Manufacturing Company. The owner's son, Sol Schwartz had insisted that Crisius operate a lathe that everyone at the plant knew was malfunctioning. Crisius was not financially compensated for the accident.

With his thumb missing and his hand bandaged Crisius could not find another job and ended up homeless, sleeping in Grant Park or fleabag hotels. It was in one of the many flea-bag hotels where Crisius met Thomas McWane.

Tommy McWaine was a drug addict from a small town near Muskegon, Michigan, and had slumbered into Chicago a few weeks before he met Crisius. The pair thought that committing robbery, would lift them out of poverty.

Crisius sent away for a mail-order gun and received it in less than a week. The pair went out on Friday, July 9, 1926 and robbed a couple out on a stroll. They got a ruby ring and twenty-eight dollars.

Just before midnight on July 10th, the pair flagged down a cab and gave Checker Cab hack, Ludwig Rose a vague destination. When the twenty-five-year old cabbie asked for a more precise terminus, he felt the end of a gun barrel against the back of his head. McWane and Crisius made Rose strip off his uniform, and hand over his cashbox. They tied him up with tire chains and tossed him into the backseat.

It was just after midnight as nineteen-year old Marie Blang sat in a car with Frederick Hein in front of her home at 1533 South 59th Court in Cicero. Hein was the superintendent of the Sunday school of the Salem Church and had given

Blang, her mother and siblings a ride home from choir practice. Blang worked as a secretary at Cracker Jacks Headquarters and taught Sunday school at her church.

McWane and Crisius pulled up next to Hein's auto, jumped out and robbed the couple of their money. Hein had the church's collection money from the evening church meeting and was shot in the head as he tried to run to the Blang home. Marie was also shot in the head and fell dead on the street.

Crisius and McWane took the dead couple's cash, jumped back into the Checker Cab and sped off. Rose still tied up in the back of the car did not like what he had heard. He managed to open the back door and jump out of the racing auto. Seeing Rose escape, the bandits stopped the car and fired their guns into him, killing him where he laid.

Driving off the pair drove recklessly through Cicero, attracting the attention of a police officer. During the pursuit, the stolen cab turned too sharply and flipped over. McWane was pinned inside, while Crisius ran off into the darkness.

On the way to jail, the police took McWane on a detour to the Cook County morgue. They showed him the lifeless, bloody body of Marie Blang who had just been received by the coroner. McWane cracked like an egg and told the police everything. He only knew Crisius as Eddy and blamed him for their crime spree. In the meantime, Crisius found a cozy nook on the roof of a three-story apartment building at 484 Quincey Street, not far from the crime scenes.

For three days Crisius hid on the roof, only climbing down to scavenge for food after dark. On the third day, he knocked on the door of the third-floor tenant, Victor Landon and asked him for food and clothing. Landon, suspecting something was severely wrong with the man shoved him out of his doorway and told him to get lost. Crisius was persistent with his demand for clothing so Landon gave him an old hat to get rid of him.

Later that day, Landon and neighbor Roy Adams notice the trapdoor leading to the roof was ajar. They found Crisius' hideout along with Rose's chauffeur's hat and coat, a watch, and a ruby ring from their earlier robbery. They also found a glove with the left thumb stuffed with paper, and a notebook filled with the semiliterate scribbling of James Crisius. Inside the notebook, police discovered what appeared to be a suicide note from the murderer.

> *Good-by, everybody. I wish you all would*
> *think it was not all my fault. The ones I killed*
> *is there (sic) own faults. I wish I had died*
> *mineself (sic) instead of the two. Oh, what a*
> *world. Never will be peace on Earth because*
> *there is (sic) too many hogs. Good Luck. My*
> *unlucky star, I will see you soon. I will see*
> *you all. So good-by, old earth…*

The heat was on and Crisius could not take the anxiety any longer. He surrendered to a cop on his beat on July 14th. Both McWane and Crisius plead guilty to the murders, although McWane pinned the murders on Crisius. The two were hopeful that by pleading guilty they would not get the death penalty. Crisius told the court his story about losing his thumb due to Sol Schwartz insistence that he use the defective lathe and then dismissing him from his job after the accident. He went on to tell the judge that he planned to murder Schwartz, but he first needed to raise money, so he could get a good attorney to represent him. To raise the money, he started a robbery spree and three innocent people were murdered in the process.

The pair received the death sentence and they were scheduled to be hanged at the Cook County Jail on New Year's Eve, 1926. McWane and Crisius spent their last day alive in their separate cells. Both were highly agitated and only ate their breakfast. McWane, visited with his family on his last night, and spoke to a minister. He spent the rest of the evening listening to a radio that was brought to his cell.

Crisius refused to see his mother and denied the request of a Catholic priest to for the Sacrament of Last Rites. At seven in the morning, on the last day of 1926, both men were led to the gallows where they quickly met their end. Hangman Harry Stanton, the official builder of scaffolds for Cook County, as well as the jail's plumber quit after the execution. "I'm 60 years old," he said. "I've had enough of this job, and I'm going out to California to take a rest." McWane's and Crisius' execution was the sixty-fifth that he had performed.

A Spotti Excuse

July 21, 1926
Benld, Illinois
Murderer - Opal Phillips
Victim-Charles Spotti, Jr.

Opal Phillips, an eighteen-year old flapper from Zeigler, Illinois showed up drunk for her job as a waitress at Charles Spotti, Jr.'s soft drink shop, aka speakeasy outside of Benld, Illinois on July 21, 1926. The twenty-four-year-old Spotti teased her about her drunkenness and Phillips replied with a chain of curse words and insults, to which the twenty-four-year old proprietor slapped her across her face.

Later that day Spotti notice his pistol was missing and asked his wife and employees if they had seen the gun. All denied that they knew anything about it. Unknown to all, Opal had taken the pistol.

A couple of hours later, Opal was still fuming over Spotti slapping her. She pulled the gun on her employer and shot him. He spent several days in the hospital, paralyzed from the neck down and died on July 25, 1926.

Opal Phillips was arrested for manslaughter and fellow employee Cora McNeal was jailed as a state witness. A tearful Phillips sobbed to the press, "I was just teasing, and it doesn't seem as if I touched the trigger. It just went off."

After sitting in the Macoupin County jail for ten weeks, Circuit Judge F.W. Burton released the young woman to her mother's custody, explaining that it would be next to impossible to get a conviction on the murder. It appeared that nobody asked what an eighteen-year old girl was doing working at a rural speakeasy, one-hundred-thirty miles from her home. Nor did anyone ask why she had taken the pistol. Nobody cared.

Opal later married and had six children. She died on June 5, 1993.

57

Oh, My Papa!

July 31, 1926
Blissfield Michigan
Murderer – John Bogar
Victims – Agnes Bogar / Amelia Bogar

When people think of Michigan, they either think of abandoned and decaying factories that once made America the economic power of the world, or the beaches of the Great Lakes, and the heavily forested and lake filled north country. The southern part of the state is largely forgotten by most people as it resembles the farm fields of Ohio, Indiana, and Illinois. This largely forgotten part of Michigan is prime agriculture land, dotted with small towns like Cassopolis, Three Rivers, Colon, Union City, Coldwater, Jonesville, Adrian, and Deerfield. They are all as forgettable as last week's grocery list.

Blissfield is one of those places. Established on the River Raison in Lenawee County in 1824 by Hervey Bliss, the town's first postmaster. The only thing that Blissfield is known for is the three parallel bridges that cross the River Raison.

John Bogar was a farmer who lived with his twenty-five-year-old daughter Agnes and her five-year-old daughter, Amelia. The circumstance of who was Amelia's father was never explained. However, Agnes had met a suiter named Frank Schwimit when she lived in Mount Pleasant. The couple were in love and Schwimit wanted to marry Agnes and adopt little Amelia. John Bogar hated Schwimit and prohibited him from seeing his daughter.

July 31, 1926 was a typical hot and humid Saturday in southern Michigan. The smell of the almost mature crops lingered in the air like incense. Frank Schwimit, along with three friends drove the grueling one-hundred-fifty miles from the college town of Mount Pleasant to the farm so he and Agnes could officially make known that they were to be married soon, but the fifty-year old Bogar would not have it. A loud argument broke out, with Bogar telling Schwimit to never come back to the

58

farmhouse. He loudly forbade Agnes from every seeing Schwimit again. His threats were loud enough for his neighbors to hear.

On Tuesday, August 3, 1926, Frank Androvitch found a note on his driveway gate that was written by his friend, Bogar, expressing that he come to his farm immediately. The letter was written in Bohemian, the mother tongue of both men.

Androvitch drove the two miles to Bogar's farm as fast as he could. Walking into the farmhouse he saw Bogar hanging by his neck in his kitchen. He immediately contacted the police, who found Agnes and Amelia dead in a bedroom. Little Amelia had been poisoned. Agnes' battered body laid in a dried pool of her own blood.

Bogar left a rambling note stating that Agnes had poisoned herself and her daughter on Friday night. He wrote that he too had taken the poison, but the effects were so slow and painful that he hung himself.

Authorities did not buy the dead man's story. After interviewing Schwimit, and his friends who accompanied him to the farm, and Bogar's neighbors, police confirmed that in a fit of rage, Bogar beat his daughter to death not long after Schwimit and his friends left on Friday evening. Feeling regret, he poisoned himself and his granddaughter, but the poison only made him sick. After four grueling nights, Bogar drove to Androvitch's farm and tacked his note on his gatepost. Bogar then drove home and hung himself.

The Phantom Killer

August 3, 1926 / May 3, 1929 / May 21, 1929 / November 25, 1935
Liberty / Kokomo / West College Corner and Anderson, Indiana
Murderer – Willard Carson
Victims – Clayton Carson / Alonzo Whalen / Charles Lawrence / Frank Levy

Every generation complains about the next generation. Lazy, selfish, rude, self-indulgent sex crazed imbeciles who expect everything to come to them easily, and with zero consequences. The older generation had to walk farther to school, in worst weather, and in sub-par clothing. The senior generation's technology was either terrible or better depending on the complainer. History is littered with ungrateful offspring, but few were as conniving and dangerous as Willard Carson.

Born in 1902, and raised on a farm outside of Liberty, Indiana farm, the only son of the law abiding and God-fearing farming couple Clinton and Minnie Carson. Willard lost interest in school and dropped out in the eighth grade. He left home not long afterwards, living in the rough and committing nuisance crimes. He was an avid reader and regular at Liberty's public library, where he checked out everything from existentialist literature to dime novels.

The population of Liberty, Indiana in 1926 was a little over one-thousand people, so an itinerant bohemian like Willard stood out like a nun at a truck stop. The only times his parents saw him is when they bailed him out of jail or when he wanted money.

The elder Clinton successfully retired from farming before he was fifty-years old and started successful cement and contracting businesses. With their daughter Glenda married, and Willard a lost cause, they moved to in a large home on an elm-lined street in the nicest neighborhood in Liberty.

Willard happily continued to live his unorthodox life. In 1926, the twenty-four-year-old slept in a forest camp outside of Liberty, spending his time drinking and reading stacks of books. He idled away his evenings in pool halls and speakeasys. Willard's lack of respect for authority, angered the small-town cops who cheerfully tossed him into jail over the slightest matter.

Things got heated on May 29, 1926 when Union County sheriff's deputy Virgil Shouse tried to arrest Carson at a Liberty pool hall for public intoxication. Carson pulled out a pistol and fired multiple rounds at the deputy who ducked for cover. Carson made his escape and disappeared like a ghost. A trait that will serve him well throughout his life.

Authorities were surprised that Carson had vanished so thoroughly. He was known to police in two states, and a dozen rural counties. It was only later that they discovered that he had a girlfriend, nineteen-year old married mother of two, Gladys Quick. Gladys had driven Willard to the nearby town of Raymond and got him on the first train out of town.

Carson soon returned to Union County and hid in a forest near his sister's farm about three miles northwest of Liberty. He built himself a secret camp complete with an improvised bed in a fork of a tree, twenty feet above the ground. Carson communicated with Quick by placing a rag on a barbed wire fence along several country roads to signal to her he was nearby.

In late July 1926, Willard approached his brother in-law, Spencer Stephen at his farm and asked for one thousand dollars. Stephen told him that he did not have that kind of money until after harvest, at which time he would give him the money. Willard told him that if he did not get the thousand dollars after harvest, he would kill him.

Furious that his parents would not help him out of his legal trouble, Willard slithered up to their home around four in the morning on a balmy and wet August 3, 1926. Using a ladder, he crept into his parent's bedroom window, and stumbled over a sewing machine, waking his parents. Clinton sat up in his bed and received four bullets from a .38 caliber revolver. One of the bullets hit Clinton in the face, one his hand and the third in his chest. Willard put the barrel of his pistol against his father's forehead and pulled the trigger one more time.

Minnie Carson escaped by climbing out a different window, running over the roof, jumping fifteen feet and injuring her back. Willard stole his father's car and began one of the oddest stories of revenge and evasion in American criminal history.

The crime shocked the small town, and a dragnet was set-up in a three-state area. The car was found about fifteen miles from Liberty, its gas tank empty. There were sightings and rumors, but the young murderer had gotten away.

It did not take long for the police to squeeze information out of Gladys Quick. She told the authorities everything, where Carson camped, where he stashed clothing and goods, and how he talked about wanting to kill his parents. She revealed to astonished police detectives that she planned to leave her husband and two children to run off with the murderer. The police tried to set-up Carson, using Quick as a lure, but he saw through the ruse and did not take the bait.

It turned out that Willard Carson had a lot of friends. The police speculated that the killer was being helped by other criminally inclined youth. The small-town police officers kicked down the doors of homes, apartments and hotel rooms as false tips flooded the station, resulting in wild goose chases and wasted resources. Word got around Liberty that Willard was going to come to his father's funeral to kill his mother even though Minnie was in a hospital with a broken back and could not attend. Nevertheless, armed men surrounded the church and cemetery during the services. Minnie never lived at her home again, opting to stay in a hotel in Liberty.

A couple of days into the manhunt, Union County hired special detectives, and posted a two-thousand-dollar reward for Willard Carson, dead or alive. Meanwhile, every crime committed in rural Indiana and Ohio was blamed on Carson. He became the boogieman of the Midwest.

On November 17, 1926, Spencer Stevens, Carter's brother in-law got the shock of his life when Willard suddenly showed up at his farm. Arriving alone, in a car, Willard curtly demanded sixty-six-hundred dollars which he claimed was his share of his father's estate. Stevens called the police as soon as his brother in-law left. Local pilots were telephoned, and several took off to look for the fugitive. Roadblocks were set up, and again, Carson vanished like a phantom.

On August 1, 1928, Carson was laying low in Kokomo, Indiana, renting a room from fifty-year old Alonzo Whalen under the name Edgar Dixon. Whalen felt there was something odd about his book reading tenant and went to the police with his suspicions. The police, along with soldiers from the Indiana National Guard showed up at the house at 639 South Union Street as quickly as they could, but it was too late, Carson was gone, but his wife Irene and their son was still there. She told police that she had met Willard in Indianapolis in November 1926 and married him not long afterwards. She had always known him as Edgar Dixon and had no idea that he was living under an alias or that he was a wanted murderer.

On the evening of May 3, 1929, Alonzo Whalen was relaxing in his favorite chair digesting his dinner and chatting with his wife. He did not know that Willard Carson was standing outside, pointing a double-barreled shotgun at him through a window. The shotgun roared, glass broke, lightbulbs were shattered, and Whalen's head was blown apart. The Phantom Killer had struck again.

Ever since the May 1926 shootout at the pool hall, Carson had been on the run. He enjoyed sending taunting letters to the Liberty police, the Union County sheriff, the Indiana State Police and various other officials around eastern Indiana. It was believed that he visited his mother often, but it was never proven. When Minnie died in 1932 there were more plainclothes police officers than family at the services. Willard did not attend his mother's funeral, but he did pop up out of the blue to his old Union County friends, usually requesting money or to forward a message.

The town of College Corner is split in half by the state lines of Ohio and Indiana. The Ohio part of the village is College Corner, while the Indiana side is called West College Corner. Surveyed in 1811, the village had high hopes for Miami University to be built there, but the school ended up being established ten miles to the southeast in Oxford. In 1929, the combined populations of both villages were less than eight-hundred people, not a large enough populace to merit a police force. Like many cities, the merchants of College Corner hired a Merchant Patrolman, a fully vested police officer whose salary is paid for by the town's shopkeepers.

Around two in the morning on May 21, 1929, Merchant Patrolman Charles Lawrence was walking the alley along the state line when he was shot in the chest with a .45 caliber pistol. Several late working merchants heard the gunshot, and one auto mechanic saw a running man, but evidently none of them had a second thought about it. At six A.M., hardware store owner Wayne Moore found the forty-three-year old's body in the alley, propped against the wall of the movie theater on the Indiana side of the alley. Lawrence's gun was about six feet away from him, and his cold dead hand clutched his flashlight.

Since the murder happened on the Indiana side of the town, the crime fell into Union County, Indiana's jurisdiction. Apparently, Lawrence and Carson knew one another, and when the daring murderer bumped into Lawrence in the dark alley, he shot the officer. Carson was well- known in College Corner, which is only eight miles from Liberty. Whether or not it was Carson who did the shooting, will never be officially known, but authorities were confident it was the Phantom Killer.

Shortly after midnight on November 25, 1935, Officer Frank Levy of the Anderson, Indiana police department approached a suspicious vehicle near the corner of 10th and John Streets. Locals in the quiet residential neighborhood had reported that the car had been idling with its headlights on in the same spot for over two hours.

As he closed his squad car door, Officer Levy, a six-year veteran of the department and father of ten children was shot four times with a .45 caliber pistol. The report of the gunshots woke up people for blocks on that cold Tuesday morning, and the police department's switchboard lit up. Assistant Chief of Police Alvin Shrinkle and Detective Jack Ryan arrived too late to plug any of the four holes in Officer Levy's chest.

A murder in Anderson, Indiana in 1935 was a big deal, and the murder of a police officer was a bigger deal. Neighbors described the car the best they could. Earl Eppley told police that a man and woman had been sitting in their car since ten that evening. No one was able to come up with a useful description.

Cons, criminals and informers in Indiana, Illinois and Ohio either took credit for the murder to enhance their criminal reputation or said that they knew who about the Phantom Killer to reduce their sentences. Janet Henderson, a young woman from Indianapolis who was suspected to be woman in the vehicle, was hooked up to a lie detector by the Indiana State Police, but she declined to answer the straight-out question, "who killed Officer Levy?"

The murders of Levy and Lawrence fit the Motus operandi of Willard Carson: A Small Midwest town, surprise attack, vanishes into the night. Carson was comfortable in small towns and cities in Ohio and Indiana where he apparently had many friends and lovers to assist his subversive lifestyle. Willard continued to write threatening letters to his sister and brother in-law over his inheritance. He also maintained his provoking communiqués with various police agencies.

The Phantom Killer managed to keep out of trouble for the next few years. When his family, and police agencies stopped receiving the predictable letters and postcards during the summer of 1939, they decided to provoke Carson into reacting. Don Stiver, Superintendent of the Indiana State Police held a press conference on November 14, 1939, to announce a renewal of a one-thousand-dollar reward for the capture of Willard Carson. Large color posters with his photo were sent to the media and law enforcement agencies throughout North America. To add salt to Willard's ego, Stilver and Willard's sister Glenda used some of the inheritance money Willard would have collected from his parent's estate as the reward.

In July 1941, Ottawa County Sheriff Frank Van Etta was having a slow day in his office in Grand Haven, Michigan. Renowned for its beautiful beaches, sand dunes and resorts, Grand Haven is still a popular summering place for residents around southern Lake Michigan. As Van Etta worked his way through police circulars, eyeing over mug shots, he came across the photo of Willard Carson, still wanted for the murder of his father fifteen years ago. Sheriff Van Etta recognized the man as Lloyd Caine, a vagrant who was found washed up on nearby beach on August 3, 1939.Clad in swimming trunks, the man had obviously drowned while swimming in Lake Michigan. Sheriff Van Etta believed the notorious undertows that Lake Michigan is infamous for pulled him underwater, swirled him around until his strength and breath ran out, and spitting him onto the beach like a cherry pit. He was buried and forgotten.

The sheriff contacted the Union County sheriff's department who sent out a detective and a team of forensic experts to Grand Haven. Glenda and Spencer Stevens also arrived in Michigan. The decayed body was exhumed and was quickly identified as Willard Carson by his well-known features; a chipped front tooth, a bullet scar, and his most peculiar attribute - a missing right pinky finger.

The reign of the Phantom Killer was over. A rich boy, turned vagabond, he assassinated his father in his own home. For fifteen years, he taunted and threatened small town police departments in rural Ohio and Indiana. As revenge for informing the police to his whereabouts, and breaking up his family, he blew the head off his former landlord almost a year later. He ruthlessly gunned down two police officers in cold blood and terrified his sister with menacing letters and unannounced visits. Had the strong Lake Michigan undertow not dragged him underwater that day, he could have continued his killings for years.

He Otto Stayed Home

August 3, 1926

Chilo, Ohio

Murderer – Raymond Ross

Victims – Otto Itin / Mamie King Metzger

Married man Raymond Ross was madly in love, but unfortunately it was not his wife that he longed for. The twenty-five-year-old farmer and tobacco agent was obsessed with thirty-two-year old Mamie Metzger, a twice divorced mother of a nine-year-old.

Early in the morning of August 3, 1926, Mamie and her nineteen-year old boyfriend Otto Itin were driving back from visiting friends in Cincinnati, thirty odd miles northwest of Mamie's home in Rural, Ohio. Just a few miles short of her home, they noticed a car following close behind them. Realizing that the tailgating car was driven by an insanely jealous Ross, Itin stepped on the gas to get away. Pulling frantically into the nearest driveway, they came to a stop in front of a farm owned by Joseph Broadwell. Ross pulled alongside of the couple and fired five shots into the car, four of those bullets hit Mamie, killing her. The fifth bullet killed the young Itin.

There are few things that will wake up a neighborhood like racing automobiles and gunshots on a Tuesday morning. Joseph Broadwell jumped out of his bed and saw Ross's auto speeding off towards the town of Felicity. Members of the Broadwell family ran to car, but the couple was quite dead.

Ross got home around daybreak. What he was doing for the previous morning hours is unknown. He admitted to his wife what he had done. Her husband's manic and erratic behavior frightened her, so she slipped out of the house the first chance that she got and hid in some shrubbery.

Clermont County Sheriff Fred Croswell and Marshall B. Edward Colvin started their investigation immediately. Questioning Mamie's friends and family, they found out that Ross was obsessed with Metzger, and that she was tired of dating the insanely jealous married man. Metzger's friends told the police that last Saturday night, at a local dance, Ross flew into a jealous rage after he saw Metzger and Itin together. He tried to drag the woman into his car but was stopped by Metzger's friends. A pistol was seen on the car's front seat.

Witnesses told the police that Ross was seen driving around the area earlier that evening. Croswell and Colvin drove to Ross's farm near Felicity, Ohio. As they knocked on the front door, they heard a muffled gunshot from inside the house. They found Ross lying dead at the tops of the stairs with a self-inflicted bullet wound in his chest.

Like a Girl Who Married Dear Old Dad

August 6, 1926
Springfield, Massachusetts
Murderer – Richard Bearse
Victim – Etta Bearse

Richard Bearse was an oddball. A graduate of Northeastern University (class of 1924), he could not get his life together. At twenty-six, he lived with his divorced mother Etta, at 25 Palmer Avenue in Springfield, Massachusetts. His father, Fred Bearse was the county treasurer for Hampden County. The two had divorced on friendly terms in 1914, with Fred generously providing for his ex-wife and son.

Richard was coddled by his parents and he grew up to be an athletic teenager, lettering in soccer, basketball and baseball at his high school. While in college he played varsity basketball. He was known as a quiet young man, who had an explosive temper.

He quit his job at the Springfield Gas Light Company in July 1926, because he felt that he could make more money with his mechanical engineering degree someplace else.

Hoping to lift his spirits, his parents sent him to Clinton Beach at Saybrook, Connecticut for a two-week vacation. While there he met Marie Wilson, a twenty-one-year-old Springfield woman. The couple fell madly in love and after two weeks of dating decided to get married the next summer.

August 5th was a Thursday, Richard, Marie and Etta went to a Springfield restaurant for dinner. The meal went well, and afterwards Richard gave his mother a ride home, while Marie met up with her sister Blanche, and a friend to go to the movies.

After Richard dropped off his mother, he met up with the girls. After the movie they took home her friend and then Blanche. The couple drove a few blocks and then parked to talk. Marie told Richard that she had been seeing someone when she met him, but she had written a "Dear John" letter to her suiter. When she showed the letter to Richard, he became visibly upset. He took Marie home and arrived back at his home around midnight.

About 6:30 A.M., neighbors heard a commotion in the Bearse home. It was severe enough that the police were called. A squad car was sent to the home, but police did not think that anything was amiss. An hour later, more sounds of violence came from the Bearse home, this time the police kicked down the door.

The police recoiled in horror at the sight of Richard Bearse, covered in his mother's blood, cradling her naked body on the intestine laden, gore covered kitchen floor. He had suffocated her, and hen revived her, only to suffocate again, her until she died. Using only his bare hands, he pulled out Etta's eyeballs, various internal organs and her heart.

Between his hysterical sobs, he told the shocked policemen, "I did it because I love her. My love was intense," and that he mutilated his mother, "to cleanse her soul from sin."

Evidence showed that Etta was first attacked in her bedroom and then dragged, probably already dead, into the kitchen. When Marie Wilson was informed of the murder, she broke down into what the newspapers called, "a nervous breakdown," and was hospitalized from her shock.

When Marie came around a few days later, she said that Richard was infatuated with her, and that he got jealous when she told him that she broke up with her former beau to be with him. She told authorities that they had discussed their wedding plans and Richard asked her if she would move into his mother's house after they got married. She told him straight out no. She felt that there was something sinister about that house.

Richard Clarence Bearse admitted to the murder and was declared insane by the court. He was locked up in the notorious Bridgewater State Hospital for the Insane for twenty-two years. He was allegedly kept in isolation the entire time.

In 1930, Fred Bearse lost the country treasurer seat that he held since 1907. He was immediately appointed the chief court clerk for Hampden County. He held the position until his retirement in 1941. Using his legal knowhow and political connections, Fred was able to get Richard Bearse retried in 1948. Richard was found "not guilty for reasons of insanity" and was committed to Northampton State Hospital, where conditions were more humane.

Richard was free to roam the grounds and to visit nearby stores. Richard Bearse was given a full pardon by Governor Robert Bradford after he was defeated for his second term and was released on March 13, 1949 to the custody of his father. He told the press that he was happy to be home. A few weeks later March 26, Fred Bearse died, leaving his son the executor of his estate.

Richard stayed at his father's home at 1075 Boston Road in Springfield for six more months before he voluntarily checked himself back into Northampton State Hospital.

Richard Bearse, who tortured and murdered his own mother, died of a heart attack at age fifty-nine on April 28, 1959, while still a voluntary patient at Northampton State Hospital.

Really Bad Dad

August 14, 1926
New Richmond, Ohio
Murderer – Scott Workman
Victim – Nora Workman

The Eighteen Amendment to the Constitution may have outlawed the sale and possession of alcohol, but it did not stop people from drinking. Instead of drinking safe and taxed alcohol, consumers were forced to drink whatever what was being sold. Tainted booze made some drinkers blind, insane or dead.

Originally from Kentucky, Scott and Nora Workman moved with their nine children to a farm outside of New Richmond, an Ohio River town in Clermont County. Even with their two eldest daughters married off, the family led a hard scrabble life. Like many farmers, Scott made moonshine in the woods near his farm to help make ends meet.

Workman stumbled into his farmhouse on Saturday morning, August 14, 1926, completely intoxicated on his moonshine. He was in an ornery mood, and angry that his teenage daughters were receiving too much attention from male suitors. Turning to his thirty-eight-year-old wife, he demanded that she stop nursing their seven-month old baby. Sitting in a chair, she ignored her drunken husband and continued nursing her infant.

Workman pulled a pistol out of his coveralls and fired three rounds at his wife, killing her with the first shot. The children screamed as their mother crumpled onto the floor.

In the commotion, eighteen-year old Margaret ran out of the house and informed the neighbors. In no time, the farmhouse was surrounded by Workman's neighbors, all armed with rifles and shotgun. As the word spread that Saturday morning, it soon turned into an army of armed and angry farmers who were not going to let Workman escape.

Workman ordered his children to help him barricade their house. Stepping onto the front porch, holding a gun and using two of his youngest children as a human shield, the Kentuckian yelled insults to the posse and fired shots into the air. Fearing that he would be lynched by his neighbors, Workman called out that he would only surrender to Sheriff Coswell. "Go ahead, shoot 'em, shoot 'em," he yelled as he tossed the wailing children up and down in his arms.

Angry men, most of them parents, gritted their teeth and wished for a clear shot that would drop Workman like a potato sack. Workman yelled, "Sure, I killed my wife. I'll kill these here too, if you shoot."

Clermont County Sheriff Fred Croswell, who by now was getting tired of the homicides his county was experiencing, arrived around eleven-thirty that morning. He quickly accessed the situation and then walked sternly up to Workman, took his pistol and marched him to his patrol car.

Later at the county jail at Batavia, Workman demanded that the sheriff take him to New Richmond, so he could see his wife's body. That request was denied.

The trial started on November 14, 1926 and was over the next day. Workman was sentenced to death at the Ohio State Penitentiary in Columbus.

Upon hearing his sentence on November 20, Workman thought that it would be good for his children, especially his teenage daughter, Frances, to be at his execution. "We'll just make a family affair out of it," said the murderer. "I want 'em all to be there. We'll get our pictures took while I'm a settin' in the chair, and then they can watch the death business."

The day of his execution, Workman ate a chicken dinner, and spent the rest of his time joking with the guards. His children either did not want to see their father electrocuted, or the authorities wouldn't allow it. It is unlikely that the now orphaned family could have raised the money for the trip to Columbus anyway.

Workman was taken from his cell on death row and led to the execution room. Reporters wrote that he had a slight grin on his face. Before he sat down, he announced to the assembled witnesses - "I took the life of my wife after we had spent many happy years together, but I did it when I was drunk and I'm not responsible. I did not know what I was doing when I shot her."

At 8:30 p.m., the switch was thrown and four minutes later, Workman was pronounced dead. It was reported that Workman's electrically charred body was shipped to Augusta, Kentucky and buried next to Nora and their three children who died in infancy. Their children were divided up among relatives to raise.

Darn those Socks

August 20, 1926
Carter Lake, Iowa
Murderer – Clayton Van Doren
Victim – Elsie "Billy" Van Doren

The Nineteenth Amendment to the United States' Constitution prohibits any United States citizen from being denied the right to vote based on their sex. It was ratified on August 18, 1920, approximately one-hundred-forty-four years after the founding of America. Currently, it seems hard to believe that women were not allowed to vote, but the staid hangover of the Victorian and Edwardian Age stuck around like the smell of cat urine on an old carpet in a windowless room.

Men and some women had a hard time accepting the changes that was happening in society. Many felt that allowing women to vote would lead to the demise of the family. There is no doubt the passing of the Nineteenth Amendment empowered American woman like nothing before. American woman from all classes exercised their rights to their individuality. Unfortunately, some men could not deal that.

On the morning of August 20, 1926, twenty-three-year-old Clayton Van Doren asked his wife to darn his socks. His twenty-five-year-old wife, Elsie, who was called Billy by her friends and family, balked at the request.

"If you don't fix these, someone else will," barked Van Doren.

"Well go ahead and get someone else," replied Billy.

Clayton, who worked as a clerk for the Union Pacific Railroad, slugged his wife on the shoulder, knocking her down the basement stairs to the first landing. He dragged her down the rest of the stairs and beat her head against the last step. To make sure that she was dead, Van Doren strangled her for at least five minutes.

He dragged her body upstairs and into the front entrance of the home. He changed his mind and dragged her into the parlor. He changed his bloody shirt and cleaned up. Wrapping the bloodstained shirt in a newspaper, he left the

75

house, stepping over Billy's battered body. He stashed the evidence into the trunk of his car and drove off to visit his aunt.

The young couple lived in an exclusive suburb called Carter Lake, Iowa. The lake was the result of the Missouri River changing course in 1870, leaving an oxbow lake on the Nebraska side of the river. Although cut off from Council Bluffs, Iowa, by the Mighty Mo and technically in Nebraska, it is to this day, still in Iowa and a neighborhood of Council Bluffs.

A few hours later he returned home with his aunt, Grace Shearer and faked surprise at finding Billy dead in the parlor of their cottage. The police took him downtown, and after four hours of interrogation in which he was "beaten, mauled, jostled and struck" by police detectives. With a split lip and a goose-egg size bump behind his right ear, Van Doren confessed to killing his wife.

The trial started on September 9, 1926, and Van Doren's attorneys John Tinleg and Richard Organ first pleaded insanity. They changed their plea to not guilty, stating that Van Doren's confession was beaten out of him. In those pre-Miranda Rights days, it was perfectly legal for police to put a suspect in a room and beat, slap and punch the accused until they confessed.

The prosecution went on with the trial, as his confession was perfectly legal at the time. The defense told the jury that the couple were wildly in love and never argued, except for the few times that he roughed Billy up. They claimed Billy accidently fell down the stairs.

Billy's sister, Emma McDowell told a different story when she testified for three-hours about her sister's relationship with Clayton. She told the court that the marriage was one of daily domestic violence and there was rarely a day in which Clayton did not quarrel with Billy. She claimed Clayton was a controlling husband who once refused to allow Billy to visit her mother's grave.

After the prosecution rested their case, Van Doren's attorney's paraded Clayton's father and a couple of Clayton's co-workers onto the witness stand to testify to Clayton's character. The defense shocked everyone by not putting the

76

defendant on the witness stand and resting their case. They explained to the jury that the prosecution did not prove their case.

The court felt otherwise and found Clayton Van Doren guilty of murder and was sentenced to life without parole at Fort Madison Prison. In 1935 his sentence was commuted to forty years by Governor Clyde Herring. On April 28, 1938 Clayton Van Doren was released on parole. On March 3, 1940, the now thirty-six-year-old Van Doren was found dead in his garage.

Jitney Bill's Cafe
August 22, 1926

San Jose, California

Murderer - William Wallace

Victim – Susie Ellish

There dozens of notable men with the name William Wallace – from the great Scotsman, to philosophers, composers, athletes, attorneys, academics, and politicians. These are men who made something of themselves. They are men who dedicated their lives to the good of humankind, country, God, or science. The William Wallace in this story does not fit into the category of great men who have that name.

Wallace was a sportsman and café owner who was active in San Jose society. The married fifty-two-year-old owned a café at 393 South 1st Street called Jitney Bill's Café. He was deeply saddened by the death of his twenty-four-year-old son earlier in the year, and conceivably transferred his grief by having an affair with Susie Ellish, a twenty-six-year old waitress and cashier who worked at Jitney Bill's.

On Sunday, August 22, 1926, Wallace's wife Rose went to Oak Hill Cemetery to place fresh flowers and tidy up her son's grave. William was to meet his wife there, but first he had to open the café at 9a.m. Wallace unlocked the café and chatted with Ellish, who was the only employee in attendance. In the solitude of the empty café, and for unknown reasons, he shot Ellish. She died instantly. Wallace left his lover lying lifeless behind the cash register counter and hopped onto a southbound streetcar full of well-dressed women and children on their way to church.

After riding twelve blocks, he pulled out his pistol, put it to his temple and blew his brains out. The streetcar came to a screeching halt as passengers in their Sunday best jumped through windows and doors to escape the carnage. Wallace died a few hours later in a hospital.

78

A Jitney Bill's customer discovered the bloody body of Susie Ellish and called the police. Perhaps Wallace heard the sirens heading to his restaurant and knew that he did not have much time left.

San Jose Police were woken out of their quiet, summer Sunday morning routine with two shootings within twelve blocks, but they put two plus two together quickly thanks to the suicide note that was on Wallace's person, It read:

> *Dear Rose: When you come down to the*
> *place this morning, everything will be over.*
> *God bless all, Bill.*

Relatives of both Miss Ellis and Wallace expressed the view that Wallace and Ellis's affair was the reason for the murder and suicide.

The Cozy Café

August 22, 1926
Shambaugh, Iowa
Murderer – Thomas Anderson
Victim – Elsie Benge

Page County Iowa sits tucked away in the far southwest corner of the Hawkeye State, sharing its southern border with the state of Missouri. The gently rolling hills and ample rain make the area perfect for agriculture. This rural county is dotted with small towns, the largest of which is the county seat, Clarinda.

Sixteen-year old Elsie Benge was from Marysville, Missouri, thirty miles southeast of Clarinda. An enterprising and perhaps cunning young woman owned her own restaurant, The Cozy Café, on North 15th Street in downtown Clarinda. One of nine children, her parents appeared unconcerned about their teenage daughter's comings and goings. Had they known that their daughter had purchased the restaurant with the help of fifty-four-year-old Thomas Anderson, perhaps they would have raised objections.

Anderson was a salesman for the U.S. Standard Stock Food Company based in Council Bluffs, Iowa, where his brother was an executive. He had no fixed address and little else was known about him, other than he had purchased the café in late June 1926, only to turn the deed over to the sixteen-year old. Together and separately, the pair bought insurance policies worth up to seven thousand dollars. Young Benge was the beneficiary of Anderson's policies.

You would have to be very naïve not to guess that Anderson was head over heels in love with Elsie. The young woman's intentions are much harder to guess. Letters that Elsie had written to her older sister Ida had stated that she could not stand Anderson. Eventually, the middle-aged salesman realized that he had been duped by someone young enough to be his granddaughter.

80

August 21, 1926 was a Saturday and Anderson was spending his morning at the Cozy Café. He was fuming at the attention that Elsie was paying to a young male customer. The ire that he held was overwhelming, as the truth of their relationship was in plain sight for all to see. Around ten, he could take no more of Elsie's flirting and spirited her out of the café and into his automobile. They were never seen alive again.

Later in the day, in Shambaugh, a hamlet a few miles south of Clarinda, three boys, Rodger Rector, Wayne Kelly and Harold Hatfield told the village police chief about a Ford Coupe that was parked on a lane in a cornfield about a mile west of town. Believing that it was a farmworker's car, the police did nothing until midnight when the boys led Officers Willis Bulknap and Earl Johnson by flashlight to the suspicious vehicle.

Seeing blood around the car and broken cornstalks, the group followed a newly made path along the edge of the field. Next to hedgerow that separated the fields, and in the trampled corn, were the dead bodies of Thomas Anderson and Elsie Benge. They were lying on a quilt, feet to feet Elsie's bruised body shown signs of a struggle. Her knees and elbows were scraped raw from when she was dragged through the field. She had been shot four times, point-blank in the chest. Powder burns surrounded each bullet hole.

Anderson, his feet touching Elsie's, had a bullet hole behind his right ear. In his right hand, clenched tightly was a .22 caliber target pistol. The couple had been dead in the hot summer sun all day. In those simpler times, it was decided right there that this was a murder/suicide. No inquest was made.

The Benge family was telephoned with the bad news. Elsie's body was claimed by her family and taken to her parent's home at 1002 E. 4th Street, in Marysville. Anderson's brother claimed Thomas' body.

Were Anderson and Benge having a sexual relationship? Why were her parents unconcerned that their sixteen-year old daughter was dating a fifty-four-year-old man? Did anyone in Clarinda wonder how a teenager, a stranger, owned and ran her own restaurant? Did Anderson get bamboozled by a mere teenager,

81

and once he realized that he had been duped of his money and dignity, murder her? Was Benge so naïve that she thought that Anderson did not want anything in return for his gifts? Nobody wanted to find out. It was probably best that there was no investigation into this crime.

Reverend Scumbag

August 24, 1926
Springfield, Missouri
Murderer – Walter Leffler
Victim – Rev. Edward Gillum

Ever since comedy was invented, in-law jokes get a reliable laugh. Mostly mother in-law jokes, but there are a few father, son, and brother in-law routines that can save a comedian from bombing. Edward Gillum was the kind of brother in-law that you report to the police.

The "Reverend" Edward Gillum was an itinerant Ozark country evangelist. Then, as now, a great many of them are con artists duping their following into giving them cash donations. Since churches are tax-exempt in the United States, there are zero oversites how the congregation's money is spent. The preacher man holding the bible high over his head with one hand is reaching into the wallets of the enthralled parishioners. Reverend Gillum was the kind of preacher who leaves town just as the parishioners are catching on to his antics. Although they say that they are servants of God, they often break eight of the Ten Commandments daily. Occasionally when these "men the cloth" break the Seventh Commandment they force others to break the Sixth Commandant.

Sometime in the early 1920's the married Gillum conned some church deacons into making him the pastor of the First Christian Church in Baker, Oregon. Gillum had encouraged his brother in law Walter Leffler, his wife Grace and their young family to move out to the high desert town to seek new opportunities. The Leffler's moved to Baker and stayed with the Gillums' in their large house.

In 1924, church deacons removed Gillum as the church pastor for dallying with several female members of the congregation. Gillum was so angered by the decision that he got into a fistfight with the clergymen in his front yard. The athletic Leffler had to hold Gillum back to stop the fight.

Shortly afterwards the Gillums' and the Lefflers' went their separate ways, with the Lefflers' moving back home to the Springfield, Missouri area. Gillum and his beleaguered wife headed back into America's heartland and went on the tent revival circuit where his high-energy sermons thrilled the money right out of the witnesses' wallets. He somehow finagled a minister position and settled into a brick and mortar church, the Christian Church of Sheridan, in Sheridan, Missouri.

For unknown reasons, he abruptly resigned from that church on August 8, 1926, after tending the souls of the village for less than a year. His wife apparently had enough of the bible-thumping con-artist went to Tulsa to "visit" her family, and Gillum bragged to anyone within earshot that he was moving to Seattle, but the preacher traveled two-hundred-eighty miles south to Springfield, Missouri, where the Lefflers' lived.

The lusty preacher had his eye on Grace since he married the couple eight years before. Inviting the family to live in Oregon was part of his ruse to have a sexual relationship with the bobbed-hair beauty. Grace could not stand the man and she stayed as far away from him as she could. After the Baker fiasco, Gillum wrote suggestive letters to Grace, who only replied to his letters out of Midwestern family courtesy.

In Springfield, Gillum made a nuisance of himself to the Lefflers', lewdly making unwanted amorous advances and writing affectionate letters to the married mother. Leffler, a contractor and well-known local boxer and athlete told his sister's estranged husband to stay away from his family, but Gillum ignored his requests and continued lurking around his home, making a pest out of himself. Gillum had a penchant for guns and always had a .22 caliber pistol on his person, and a .22 rifle in his automobile.

On August 24, 1926, Leffler came home from work only to find his shifty brother in-law, lazing in the front room of his house at 1924 Pierce Avenue. Grace was hanging up laundry in the backyard, staying far away from the unwelcome in-law.

84

Leffler, doing his best to be diplomatic, told Gillum that he was not welcome at his home. Gillum told him to mind his own business and reached into his pocket. Thinking that Gillum was going for his pistol, Leffler picked up an Indian Club, that he used for exercising, and hit Gillum in the forehead with it. Gillum crashed through the front window of the house, landing on the porch. Fearing for his life, Leffler hit him two more times in the head with the club.

Leffler, stunned by what had occurred, ran a few blocks to a grocery store that had a telephone. An ambulance took the bloodied Gillum to the hospital while the police took Leffler into custody.

While riding in the police car, Leffler told the officers, "I didn't mean to kill him. I only meant to teach him a lesson, so he would stay away from my wife and my home and stop trying to cause trouble" Twenty-seven-year old Grace Leffler tried to calm her husband stating, "Honey, I am sorry you had to do this, but I knew twelve months ago that you would have to kill Gillum."

The forty-year old Gillum was pronounced dead of a fractured skull at eleven o'clock that evening. Greene County prosecuting attorney, Harold Lincoln, who earlier in the year, had to deal with a double murder, and police standoff by Clinton Hollingsworth, probably wondered aloud what the heck was wrong with his town, kept Gillum in custody while they sorted out what had happened.

Leffler had no problem telling the officials about his obnoxious brother in-law's infatuation with his wife. "Gillum has threatened to kill me many times," he told Greene. "He has even written me a letter in which he threatened my life. For a long time, he has been trying to bring about an estrangement between myself and my wife and relatives. He has tried to be intimate with my wife and I had warned him repeatedly to stay away from my home."

Instead of being reasonable, the bullying Gillum would appear at his home during all hours, especially while he was at work. He was intent on having a sexual relationship with Mrs. Leffler, who rejected all his advances. Because of the gun that Gillum always carried, as well as the personal threats that he had made, Leffler had every reason to believe that Gillum would kill him.

"I don't care what's done in the case, only I want justice. When I came home Tuesday evening, Gillum was in the front room, and my wife was in the backyard gathering clothes. I spoke to Gillum in a friendly way and he replied, 'Now Leffler, mind your own business.' At this time, he reached for hip pocket and I thought he was after a gun. I picked up an Indian club which was lying on the floor near me and struck him in the head, twice before he fell and once after. I just went crazy mad, I guess."

On September 1, 1926, prosecuting attorney Lincoln dismissed the charges explaining that Leffler had killed Gillum while protecting home and family.

Plantation Assassination

Wetumpka, Alabama
August 30, 1926
Murderers – Clyde Bachelor / Hayes Leonard
Victim - Lamar Smith

Wetumpka, Alabama is about as deep as you can get into the American South. The town was settled by the second and third sons of Carolina and Virginia plantation owners after General Andrew Jackson depopulated the area of Creek Native Americans in 1814.

Land was in short supply in the Carolinas as big plantations, worked by African slaves, took up most of the available property. Plantations would be inherited by the eldest son, leaving his brothers without property, so before the embers cooled in the Creek natives' campfires, young rich men scrambled to get a piece of the fertile land. To farm the land, the newcomers needed slaves, so the men's father's or eldest brother sold at reduced prices, their most troublesome and uppity slaves.

Without any restrictions on the treatment of slaves, and without the scorning eyes of "proper" slave owners, the plantation owners of the Deep South became known for their brutality. Uncooperative slaves in the Southeast were threatened to be sold and sent to the Deep South.

The practice of slavery stopped when General Robert E. Lee surrendered to General Ulysses S. Grant at Appomattox Courthouse, Virginia on April 9, 1865. Former slaves and their offspring were treated as subhuman. It was in this environment that Hays Leonard was forced into a murder.

Former Elmore County Probate Judge Lamar Smith and his wife Sallie had gotten home after a long day of work and socializing on August 30, 1926. It was typical hot, muggy summer night in the Deep South, and the judge laid down on his bed to read the newspaper and relax. Suddenly the stillness of the evening was interrupted by a blast of buckshot from a 12-gauge shotgun. Parts of Judge Smith's skull and brains were splattered into a wall. Stunned, and hit by buckshot, Sallie ran out of her home as fast as she could.

Sallie injured and covered in blood, her own and the judge's, stumbled onto the street and into the arms of neighbors. The loud shotgun had thundered through the quiet streets of Wetumpka, which in 1926 had a population of fifteen-hundred people.

Someone saw a strange car parked a block away, under a pecan tree. An ambulance was called for Judge Smith, but he died with half of his brain exposed, a few minutes later. Almost immediately the police had two suspects and fearing a lynching, the Elmore county sheriff's deputies and Wetumpka police took the prisoners by motorboat to Montgomery, and a proper jail.

The suspects were not the usual ones. Twenty-five-year-old Caucasian Clyde Bachelor, a local entrepreneur with deep family roots in the area. He was also the son in-law of Judge Smith. The other suspect was twenty-six-year-old Hayes Leonard, an African American sharecropper who lived on the Bachelor family plantation. The two men knew each other for most of their lives. Bachelor spilled his guts to the police telling them he was failing financially and was desperate for some ready cash. He figured that his wife would inherit his in-law's estate and he would once again be fiscally solvent. He pointed at Leonard, and told the officers, "That old Negro fired the shot, but I made him do it."

Elmore County was in an uproar. One of the most respected members of the community was gunned down in his own bed, and his beloved elderly wife injured through the prompting of their daughter's husband. These kind of things happened to poor Negros and uneducated hillbillies, not upstanding prominent old established families like the Bachelors' and the Smiths'.

The Sixth Amendment to the Constitution guarantees the right to a speedy trial, and that is exactly what Bachelor and Leonard got. The trial started on September 7, one week after the shooting. Charged with murder and attempted murder,

Bachelor was tried first. He was driven from Montgomery by Sheriff John Golden and three other heavily armed police officers. Their route was kept secret to avoid interference from vigilantes. On the advice of the expensive attorneys that the Bachelor family hired he entered a plea of not guilty by reason of insanity.

Because Bachelor had confessed, it was the only way for him to avoid a death sentence. Hayes Leonard was the first person called to the stand. Although Leonard was only in his mid-twenties, everyone referred to him as an old Negro. William Hinds Jr., a United Press correspondent described Leonard as, "a powerful negro with an animal-like face and little evidence of intelligence."

When Judge Smoot informed Leonard that he did not have to testify if he did not want to, Leonard replied, "Yes sir, boss. I'd like to tell the truth." Leonard told the entire story how Clyde Bachelor bullied Leonard, who rented farmland from the Bachelor plantation into committing the crime by offering to pay off his car, forgive his debt for that season's fertilizer, and four-hundred dollars cash.

They tried twice to kill the Smiths. The first time Leonard went to the Smith house in the guise of a telegraph deliverer, but once the Judge came to the door Leonard pretended that he forgot the message. The second time, Bachelor poisoned the Smith's pet dogs and left the doors open so Leonard could get inside undetected. He stood in the house with a club, but could not get the nerve to kill Mrs. Smith when she entered the room that he was hiding in. He ran out of the house.

Finally, on August 30, 1926, Bachelor got a shotgun and gave it to Leonard, telling him to shoot the old man through the open window as he reclined on his bed reading the newspaper. Bachelor sat in his car, twenty yards away under a pecan tree.

The defense then called several business associates, and his brother in-law, George Smith to testify if they had ever seen Clyde Bachelor behave in an odd manner. All of them replied that with the exceptions of paying his bills late, they had never seen Clyde Bachelor do or say anything abnormal. Others called to the stand were Willie Rawls, who saw Bachelor's car parked near the Smith home,

Sheriff John Golden and other deputies who witnessed Bachelor's confession, and three doctors who were called to the home after the shooting.

Clyde's brother W.E. Bachelor testified in his brother's defense that Clyde had been acting strangely for the last year, and that he had been having convulsions.

After thirteen hours of deliberation, the jury came back with the verdict of guilty. When asked by the judge if he had anything to say, Bachelor answered, "What good would words do now?" Bachelor was immediately sentenced to death, with the date set on October 22, 1926. Judge Smoot ended his judgment with, "May God have mercy on your soul." It was the first time in Elmore County history that a judge applied the death penalty on a member of a wealthy and prominent family.

Because Hayes Leonard admitted his guilt, his trial was skipped, and he was sentence to death the same day as Bachelor, but both men had reprieves. Governor Bibb Graves' office was swamped by letters asking that Leonard's life be spared because of his low intellect and his inability to understand the seriousness of the charges. Governor Graves commuted Leonard's execution and gave him life in prison.

The Governor, who was a friend of both the Smith and the Bachelor families, visited Clyde in prison the day before he was to be executed. Clyde's wife Elizabeth refused to allow him to see their three-year old son Henry, while he was on death row. She left the state to avoid publicity; however, the Governor ordered that the child be brought to the prison to see his father for the last time. He gave the boy a long hug, without saying a word, then told the warden to take the boy away. Bachelor pleaded with the governor to spare his life, but the governor told him that he could not. He was to die shortly after midnight on July 15, 1927.

Dressed in loose fitting white prison clothing, and his head shaved, Bachelor was led into the execution room. He shook hands with his brother Elmer and two of his cousins but said nothing. A minister led a prayer and sang, "Have Thy Way." Bachelor sang along. Still singing, he sat down in the electric chair while attendants strapped him down, applied electrodes to his bare skin and attached the helmet on his head.

90

The guards waited until the hymn was finished. Bachelor turned his head and smiled at Warden Shirley, who threw the switch. Bachelor stiffened from the jolt and his exposed skin turned purple. After thirty seconds the electricity was cut. A doctor checked for a heartbeat and nodded. Another thirty seconds of electricity was shot through Bachelor's body. This time it killed him. He was buried in the family cemetery on the Bachelor Plantation.

Newspapers took note that this was a turning point in race relations in the Deep South. It was the first time that a white person was executed, while a black person, who committed the actual crime was spared.

Life of Crime

September 25, 1926
St. Louis, Missouri
Murderer - Thomas Lowry
Victim - Officer Eugen Lovely

St. Louis motorcycle officers Eugene Lovely and Thomas J. Jones started their Saturday morning shift a little differently on September 25, 1926. For reasons lost to time, they were assigned to ride in a police car, instead of their motorcycles.

Around noon, the officers spotted a speeding automobile at Delmar Boulevard and North Sarah Street and gave chase. With the siren blaring and lights flashing, the officers chased the car through largely residential neighborhoods for three miles. At the intersection of Lindel Boulevard and Kings Highway Boulevard, in front of the Chase Park Plaza Hotel, Officer Lovely finally got the speeder to pull over.

As the officers got out of their squad car, twenty-one-year old Thomas Lowry jumped from the driver's seat and shot the twenty-four-year old Lovely in the head. As Officer Jones turned to run, Lowry fired, hitting Jones in the ankle. Officer Jones managed to get a shot in, hitting Lowry in the arm as he escaped through an alley, where he carjacked an auto and made his getaway.

Police found Lowry's jammed semi-automatic pistol and his jacket, which had extra ammunition in a pocket near the scene of the crime. Blood and a bullet hole confirmed that the shooter was wounded.

The two passengers who were riding with Lowey were thirty-eight-year old Louis Fagin and his four-year-old daughter, Rose. Fagin immediately told the police who the shooter was. He later said, probably after getting beat up in an interrogation room at police headquarter, that he and Lowry were involved in running liquor between Chicago and St. Louis.

Police quickly discovered that Lowey who had once worked for the Post Office, had serve one year of a two-year prison sentence for burglary, and thought the police were after him for a stolen car he had already gotten rid of. What Lowry did not know is there was an All-Points Bulletin out for five men who robbed a bank in Festus, a town about forty miles south of St. Louis. The St. Louis police were expecting the robbers to come to the city.

The Chief of Police Joseph Gerk put a thousand-dollar reward for Lowry, dead or alive, and the greater St. Louis Metro area was all eyes and ears to collect the rewards. Meanwhile Lowry was hiding out at a friend's house in Pine Lawn, a village just northwest of St. Louis.

Around nine that evening, police burst into Lowry's hideout with guns blazing. They found the wounded Lowry hiding behind a phonograph player, which in 1926 was the size of a kitchen stove.

At his trial he told the court that he shot Officer Lovely because he was suspected of being involved in the robbery of a Grand Trunk Railroad mail car on September 10, 1926 near Evergreen Park Illinois. "I had to do it," he explained. "I'm wanted for another job." This did not endear him to the jury.

Lowry was found guilty on February 25, 1927 and sentenced to death.

Newspapers reported that Lowry seemed stunned by the verdict and did not seem to believe what happened to him. "I don't know what to say now," Lowry told reporters after the trial ended. "They sure put it over me in a hurry. It's been a bum deal. I don't know whether to make an appeal or not."

After the usual appeals, the noose became clear. Lowry was ordered to be executed on February 1, 1929 at the St. Louis City Jail. He was to be hung simultaneously with another murderer, Leonard Yeager, who shot innocent bystander, Conniours Schou during a botched robbery.

February 1, 1929 was a brutally cold day in St. Louis, with temperatures near zero. Lowry and Yeager were brought to the sixth floor of the city jail where the nooses hung. The trap door opened to the fifth floor, where their necks would break from the fall. At 6:15 a.m., five guards pushed five buttons. Only one of the buttons would open the trapdoor.

Bed's On Fire

October 16, 1926

Spavinaw, Oklahoma

Murderer – Unknown

Victim – Leonard Floyd Greer

By all accounts Leonard Greer was a drunk, something he kept from his wife Anita Dunham until after their January 4, 1914 wedding. It was not unusual for Leonard to go on multi-week benders, as his binges did not interfere with his job as a salesman for a hydraulic valve company.

Anita was born in Oklahoma, but raised in Birmingham, Alabama, where she was given a good upbringing and education. As a proper southern woman, Anita was also a Sunday school teacher. She did everything that she could to help her husband with his alcohol problem.

The couple moved around a lot, partially because of Leonard's occupation and mostly because Leonard's drunkenness sometimes caused him to lose his job. Between 1914 and 1924, the pair lived in Green Bay, Sioux Falls, Brownsville, and Oklahoma City before Leonard opened a sporting goods, auto accessories and repair garage in the resort town of Spavinaw, Oklahoma.

In 1921, Lake Spavinaw was formed by damming Spavinaw Creek to provide drinking water for Tulsa, fifty-five miles to the southwest. The fishing was excellent, and people flocked to the lake to relax. The Greer's were at the right place at the right time and their business flourished. Their store sold bait, and fishing gear, and anything that one would need for a lakeside vacation.

The couple lived in a cottage behind the shop. Business was good enough that Greer had to hire salespeople, mechanics and clerks. Leonard left the managing of the store to Anita, and their employees, while he fished and drank himself into a stupor. By noon the thirty-five-year-old was usually passed out in his bed, which was fine with Anita and her employees. When Leonard was conscious, he was belligerent and domineering and created problems when nothing was wrong. Everything ran smooth at the shop, if Leonard was passed out or away.

One of the store's employees was Ben Schuh, a tall, thin, blonde veteran of World War One. The thirty-four-year-old worked for the Greer's as a mechanic. He was a gentle and intelligent man from Varina, Iowa, whose ill health was probably war related. In a nutshell, Ben was everything that Leonard was not.

Anita and Ben were kindred souls, and they enjoyed each other's company. Ben would often drive with Anita to Tulsa to order more merchandise for the store. They would usually take all day to complete the one-hundred-forty-mile round trip.

Stopping to sightsee and shop. Other employees and the townspeople thought that the two were having an illicit affair. Certainly, Anita and Ben were fond of each other, but Anita was known as a dedicated wife.

In mid-October 1926 Schuh and Leonard had a disagreement, and Schuh quit his job at the garage. Schuh, who lived at the Case Hotel, informed the proprietor of the hotel that he was going back home to Iowa. He planned on driving his Ford Roadster he five-hundred miles back, even though the roads were mere wagon trails in 1926.

On Saturday, October 16, 1926, Schuh met up with his former co-workers for breakfast at a Spavinaw café and appeared to be in good spirits. On his way out of town, he stopped at Anita's shop. He asked clerk Myrtle Miller if Anita was awake yet. Miller went to check, and Anita came out to meet Schuh. They sat on the porch of the cottage and chatted while Leonard was passed out in his bed in a nearby room. The two had an emotional goodbye, and tears were shed as Schuh drove off.

At around seven that evening, the lights went out at the Greer compound. A minute later a fire started in the Greer's bedroom. Anita found her unconscious husband on the burning bed. A broken light bulb hung over the bed. Throwing cups of water to extinguish the flames, the panicked woman dragged the deadweight drunk out of the blaze. She was soon joined by Miller, her brother

95

Jesse, and employees Andrew Walker and Louie Wickliffe, who put the fire out and carried Leonard into the store.

Doctor Case, who owned a hotel was across the street, was summons. The doctor could tell immediately that the man was dead, as his forehead had a hole in it as if he was hit by a heavy object like a hammer or the butt of a pistol three or four times.

Mayes County Sheriff Charles M. Kelly arrived at the scene and tried to make sense of the situation. With only a population of a couple hundred, everyone in Spavinaw knew Leonard was a blackout drunk, and everyone knew of the affection that Anita and Ben shared. A large percentage of the population was in one way or another employed by the couple and liked them.

When the sheriff found out that Schuh had left town twelve hours earlier, the dim-witted country lawman put two and two together and came up with five. An all-point- bulletin went out for Schuh, who was found at his family home in Varina, Iowa. Anita Greer was also arrested and held separately at the Mayes County Jail until a Grand Jury could decide on charges.

Schuh and Greer both said that they were innocent. Schuh wanted desperately to see Anita, but she did not want anything to do with him. It was bad enough that her husband was murdered, but to be charged with killing him was too much for Anita. Leonard may have been a useless drunk, but he was her husband for twelve years.

Anita's father and sister came for support, as did Schuh's legal team from Iowa. Anita made bail after the charges were brought and went back to running her store. Schuh was denied bail, and by the start of his trial on March 13, 1927, looked every bit of a man who had been in jail for five months.

Defending Schuh was J.H. Langley and A. Lee Battenfield, both capable attorneys who brought along Doctors W.R. Marks and Charles Near. With Judge A.V. Coppedge presiding, the state's case was led by Mayes County Attorney W.W. Powell and Leonard's brother in-law E.H. Johnson, a gray-haired, old school country attorney from Harlan, Kentucky.

There was confusion about how Schuh returned to Iowa. Witnesses claimed that Schuh stopped in Vinita, a town twenty miles north of Spavinaw, stored his Ford Roadster there, and bought a train ticket to Iowa. His train did not leave until two in the morning on Sunday. This was never proven.

Captain Sealls, the watchman at the Spavinaw boathouse testified that Schuh had come by the day before he left town and asked for a hammer that he had lent him. Nothing unusual about that, as Schuh was a mechanic, but to the prosecution, a ballpeen hammer may have been the murder weapon.

Louie Wickliffe's testimony was tossed by the prosecution because he was evasive and unwilling to testify. The young African American was sweated out on the stand until he admitted that he had been driven to the trial from Vinita by Rollie Clark, an attorney representing Anita Greer.

Jesse Miller told the court that he went with Schuh to buy some whiskey the day before the murder. The transaction took place in a cemetery. Afterwards they drove to Greer's store, where Anita appeared on the back porch dressed in a night gown and kimono. The pair spoke for fifteen minutes on the porch in full view of her employees Andrew Walker, Louie Wickliffe, Jesse and Myrtle Miller. Andrew Walker was embarrassed by the defense when during his testimony he admitted that he had a date with a woman the night before Greer was killed. He was asked if his wife knew about it, and Walker turned red with embarrassment, grinned and said that he hoped that she never would.

Dr. Chase testified that Anita told him that she found him at eight in the evening, when she brought him some water. Chase also stated that he believed that Greer had been dead for more than several hours. Schuh's attorneys ripped the physician's opinion to shreds and mocked his abilities. Blisters were formed on the body and a heated argument broke out over Dr. Chase's skills as a doctor as he did not know that skin cannot blister after death.

Asking Dr. Chase if besides being a medical doctor was, he also the cook at his hotel? Chase replied, "Yes, I am a cook, and I'm proud of it. It takes more brains to cook than to be a lawyer or a doctor." Doctor Chase was laughed out of the courtroom.

The charred bed, complete with bloody sheets, blankets and pillows was set up in the courtroom to allow Sheriff Charles Kelly to show the court how he found the body, completely forgetting that the Greer's body had been moved into the store.

Powell introduced letters written by Schuh to Anita while he was in Iowa some of which indicated that he hoped that Anita would be with him soon. The defense retorted, "As for this love stuff," said Battenfield, "let me tell you about it. It's as old as Adam and Eve. If you are going to convict every man in Oklahoma who has an illicit love affair, you will depopulate the state."

Pulling at straws, the prosecution brought to light that there was a possibility that Schuh had lied on his divorce decree from his former wife Mildred, that he had been a resident of Oklahoma when he was a non-resident. It was a pointless tactic to make Schuh seem more unlikeable.

The case presented by the state relied entirely on circumstantial evidence. The state provided no evidence that Schuh was at the scene when the killing occurred.

The jury of eleven farmers and one carpenter had to decide on three things. The first was whether Schuh made a pact with Anita to murder her husband so that the couple could continue their romantic relationship? Second, did Schuh purchase whiskey knowing that Leonard would drink it until he passed out, making it easier to murder him by bashing his head with a hammer? Thirdly, did Schuh leave Spavinaw the morning of the murder to provide a cover for his actions?

It only took a few hours for the jury of hicks to come back with a guilty verdict.

Anita Greer's trial started a few days later March 23, 1927, with attorney J. Howard Langley representing Anita. For the state the same judge, country attorney, as well as Anita's brother in-law.

E.H. Johnson helped the prosecution. The fire and brimstone spouting Johnson opened the trial demanding that Anita receive the death penalty. "You are red-blooded men," Johnson said. "Of the two punishments I am sure you would deal out to this woman the mild. If you are to speak a warning to married women who error with your verdict and if that verdict must be guilty then send Anita Greer to the electric chair."

Jesse Miller testified that he and his sister Myrtle went along with Anita and Schuh to a Negro picnic in Tulsa. Anita and Schuh sat in the car most of the time and appeared to be kissing. "Ben had his arm around Mrs. Greer, and I believe they were kissing, but I can't say for sure about that. Anyway, they had their heads real close together."

Myrtle Miller went on the stand and repeated what she said when she testified at Schuh's trial. She went on about the trips to Tulsa and how close the couple appeared. When asked what Anita said when her husband was discovered dead, the eighteen-year old replied that Anita said, "Oh, I am so glad Ben is out of town," He would surely be accused of this."

Andrew Walker testified that Greer had been intoxicated for several days before his death. "The last time I saw Greer alive was on Friday, October 15, the day before his body was found. We had been out of town to buy a quart of whisky, and I took him a glass of ice water in his home."

Vinita morticians Louis Rogers, E.E. Clinger and C.A. Wright testified they agreed that Greer had been dead only a couple of hours by the time they arrived. They stated his body was still warm when they took him to the funeral home.

Greer's former employer, L.P. Murray of Minneapolis testified that Greer was an incurable drunkard when he worked as a salesman for his tool company. He had known him several years and witnessed Greer growth from being a moderate drinker to a habitual drunkard.

On March 29, 1927 Anita Greer's attorney J. Howard Langley compared her marriage to Leonard as a love triangle with John Barleycorn. "At any time, you want to force Leonard's choice between us I am ready, said John Barleycorn," shouted the attorney. "Already Leonard had chosen between them," Langley continued. "He loved John Barleycorn more than Anita, but she did not turn from her husband for this infidelity. She clung to him, worked for him, ministered to him in the illness, which was excessive drink had brought upon him."

Anita took the stand for four hours. She was described in the newspaper as comely, pale with black bobbed hair. She replied to the question in a listless manner. Anita told the court about her twelve years of marriage to Leonard, and his drunken sprees that would last for weeks. His alcoholism was so bad that a doctor instructed her how to use a hypodermic needle to inject him with a lifesaving potion. She spoke of the frequent moves, lost jobs and financial stress due to his perpetual alcohol consumption. She told the court that a doctor told her Leonard would die within a few years if he kept up his drinking. She wept softly into a handkerchief while she described the death scene.

The only solid evidence was the love note on a piece of cardboard that was written in Schuh handwriting that said, "I love you." The love letter from Schuh expressed hope that Anita could come to Varina, so they could marry before Anita was too old to have children.

W.W. Powell asked for the death penalty during the five-hour closing argument, with the victim's brother in-law, E.H. Johnson putting his two-cents worth just to make the trial more appealable.

After four hours of deliberation, the jury voted to acquit Anita Greer. Surrounded by her father, sister and the defense team, Anita wept. She told the press that she was going to go back home to Alabama with her father and sister.

Schuh appealed the verdict, and on September 14, 1929, the Oklahoma Supreme Court granted him a new trial. The state failed to show a definite conspiracy and all testimony in that connection was circumstantial. There was also an affidavit from jury member Lester Downum of Salina who stated that he was convinced of Schuh's guilt before he was accepted for jury duty. A second affidavit was by Mrs. Walter Riley, who said she overheard Downum declare in a Salina barber shop, prior to the trial, he was going to be on the jury that would try Schuh, and that he intended to "pour it on" both.

The appeal was also concerned that Jessie and Myrtle Miller were coerced by Sheriff Kelly, as they had both stayed at the private home of the sheriff before and during the trial. In a nutshell, the state had no case.

Schuh had suffered a stroke while in prison and remained in ill health during the appeal. He was described as a fragile ghost. Mayes County declined to retry Schuh.

Whatever Anita and Ben had together was lost in the American legal system, and he returned to Iowa in poor health, eventually entering the Western Branch of the National Home for Disabled Volunteer Soldiers in Leavenworth, Kansas in 1934.

In 1937 he married Ada Schaufler and adopted her two children from a previous marriage. He died at the Veterans Hospital in Wadsworth, Kansas on July 6, 1947.

In July 1929, Anita Greer sued the Commercial Travelers of America Company to collect sixty-three hundred dollars of insurance money for the death of Leonard.

Instead of going back home to Alabama, Anita stayed in Spavinaw, and kept the bait store/filling station running. In 1930, she married C.E. Peck in Rogers, Oklahoma. By 1940, she was still living in Spavinaw, and worked as kitchen helper in a café. In 1951, she married Boyd M. Craven in Sonoma, California. She died on August 29, 1969 in Spavinaw.

Nobody will ever know who killed Leonard Greer. There is a theory that it may have been a robbery committed by outlaws who inhabited the nearby Cookson Hills, where generations of criminals had found safe refuge from the law. Since Spavinaw did not have a bank, and the receipts from the day, a busy Saturday, were kept in a closet in the room where Leonard was murdered. Perhaps Leonard slipped out of his alcohol induced coma and discovered the robbery in progress and he was hit in the head with either a hammer or the butt of a handgun to shut him up. The fire was started to cover up the evidence. Poor detective work and a bias prosecution made the case unsolvable. However, if Ben and Anita committed the crime, they got away with murder.

Prairie Madness
November 15, 1926
Scotland, South Dakota
Murderer - Walter Zweifel
Victims – Mrs. John Grosz / Robert Zweifel

The tediousness of the Great Plains can have unnerving effects on people who live there, day in and day out, year after unchanging year. The monotony of the landscape, the ever-present wind whistling through everything with a crack can cause serious mental instability in some people. From the earliest pioneers losing their minds to modern days, the isolation, vastness, and unrelenting skies can tip an already unstable person into full blown murderous insanity.

Southeastern South Dakota is flat and featureless. Sparely populated and horizon to horizon the view is corn and soybeans as far as the eye can see. It is hot and humid in the summer, and as cold as the artic in the winter, with little to break the wind rushing down from Canada. In 1926, the region was all dirt roads and weathered buildings, reminiscent of the first twenty minutes of the 1939 classic film, The Wizard of Oz.

Twenty-nine-year-old Walter Zweifel was trying to get ahead in life. He did what was expect of his kind and married a girl, whose first name is not mentioned, from a neighboring farm. Together they had two children. They were obedient family members and devoted in-laws. When it came time for his wife's father to start dividing his various and vast property holdings among his children, Walter's wife was left out of the will.

Most of the citizens of Bon Homme County, South Dakota were immigrants from Eastern Europe - Czechs, Germans, Ukrainians, and Poles who came to America by the hundreds of thousands to escape the hellhole that was central Europe in the 1880's.

The railroads were offering tracks of land for sale in the Dakotas at attractive prices, and hordes of Scandinavians and Eastern Europeans settled on the land that turned out to be less than the brochures said. The immigrants struggled; the less successful ones sold their land to neighboring farmers or relatives and moved somewhere else. Over time farms grew to thousands of acres and large cash crops like corn and wheat could be profitably grown.

Large families were the norm at the time because their free labor was needed to run the farm. It was not unusual for six or eight children in one family and they all helped as soon as they could walk. They spoke their parent's mother tongue, and sometime did not learn English until they were ten or eleven. It did not matter much because the immigrant's offspring where needed on the farm. They did not need any further education. They were basically indentured cultural slaves to the Old World. Family and God were the order of the day, and you had any ideas of your own, it was beaten out of you before you had a chance to dream about it.

It is unknown if old man Grosz gave anything to Zweifel and his unnamed wife, or if Zweifel thought they deserved more. There was tension with his mother in-law, whose first name is unknown, and his twenty-four-year-old brother in-law Emmanuel Grosz. They allegedly told Zweifel in 1925 that he and his wife would never receive any property from the Grosz family. Why they would treat their daughter and her husband so unfairly is unknown. Perhaps there was some old-world prejudice, with the Grosz family being from Poland and Catholic, and the Zweifel family from Germany, and probably Lutheran.

Life went on for a year for Zweifel, the harvest was brought in, the holidays occurred, spring planting, graduations, birthdays, marriages, the Fourth of July, all of life's rich pageants that families celebrate among themselves where attended by Zweifel with his extended family.

The weather on Monday, November 16, 1926 was brisk, but tolerable. At the Grosz house a friendly game of cards was the evening entertainment. Setting up in the summer kitchen, twenty feet from the main house was Emmanuel, his brother Solomon's wife, neighbors twenty-year old Robert and fourteen-year old Clarence Zweifel, Walter's younger brothers.

Walter Zweifel crept up to the summer kitchen, not knowing that his two brothers were inside. He stuck an old double-barreled, hammer and breach shotgun up to a window and fired, shattering Robert's skull. Hearing the report of the gun, Mrs. Grosz ran out of the main house's kitchen and into Walter's line of fire. He shot her squarely in the chest, killing her instantly.

As the wounded ran out of the summer kitchen, Walter reloaded and fired at his fleeing relatives. He was specifically after Emmanuel, who he chased a quarter of a mile through a cornfield, firing and reloading the ancient gun as he ran.

None of the wounded knew who the shooter was. They certainly did not think it would be kin. Authorities were called, and police and ambulances arrived. In the rural tradition, neighbors from miles around converged on the crime scene to see if they could help.

Walter Zweifel knew that the jig was up when his wife got the phone call with the news that her mother and brother in-law were murdered. He drank an unidentified poison and crawled into his bed, refusing to go with his wife to the crime scene – the house she grew up at. Believing that he was dying,

Walter waited until his wife left and called the Sheriff Koenig to admit to the crime. He coldly confessed, telling the sheriff he made up my mind to kill Mrs. Grosz and Emmanuel Grosz last summer because the other children were given farms and homes. The sheriff called an ambulance and drove like a madman to the Zweifel farm. It was not too late, and Walter was taken to a hospital where his life was saved.

Walter Zweifel plead guilty and was giving a life sentence all within sixty-six hours after the murders. He was still suffering from the effects of the poison and would have benefited if he had an attorney representing him.

Zweifel entered the state prison in Sioux Fall, and immediately refused to eat or talk. When the guards could get him out of his cell, he would break free and run back into his cell. He was in obvious need of medical attention, as well as a mental health specialist.

On November 25, 1926, nine days after he murdered his brother and mother in-law, Walter Zweifel was found dead in his cell. He had died from the poison. His parents came to claim his body but could not afford to retrieve it. He was given to a medical school in Vermillion, South Dakota per South Dakota law.

Straight To Hell

November 17, 1926

South Torrington, Wyoming

Murderer - Reverend J.B Minort

Victims – Herbert Minort / La Von Minort / David Minort / Clarence Minort and Mrs. Minort

J.B. Minort was a man of redemption. He was once a rebellious man, who served seven years in a Missouri prison for second degree murder. Along with several other men, he was arrested in 1904 for the robbery and murder of an old miner in Riverton, Missouri. The old man's head was split with an axe for five-hundred dollars. Like many men behind bars, he found God and became a Baptist minister after he served his time. He married, raised a family of five and eventually after stints in various Midwestern parishes including some years in Alliance, Nebraska, became the pastor of the First Baptist Church in South Torrington, Wyoming, where he also managed a grain elevator.

The Reverend was widely respected for his pro-labor union views and he had acquired a large congregation among the Baptists along Highway 26 in western Nebraska and Eastern Wyoming.

Because of his work with labor causes, Wyoming Governor William B. Ross, a Democrat, appointed him the State Commissioner of Child and Animal Protection on July 22, 1924. The post was taken away from him on November 8, 1924 when he was accused of transporting two young women over Wyoming state line to Scottsbluff, Nebraska for immoral purposes.

The trio had checked into a hotel room, after which Minort left town, stranding the young women in Scottsbluff. The charges were dropped when the two young women could not be found to testify.

With those charges behind him, and his reputation a little worse for wear, the Reverend remained popular at the First Baptist Church. He was a staid member of the Democratic Party and his support was sought after by other Democratic

106

politicians. He became a police judge for the town of Torrington leveling fines of traffic violators. Little did Minort know that being the Justice of the Peace for a little dusty farming community would lead to such disastrous results.

On November 7, 1926, Torrington resident Dick Armstrong was in Bayard, Nebraska, fifty-four miles southeast of Torrington when he spotted the Reverend in a hotel with a woman who was not his wife. Armstrong was angry at Minort for fining him for having nonfunctioning lights on his automobile.

Armstrong lived up to his first name and informed the police about the adulterous rendezvous. Once again, he was charged of violating the Mann Act and was released on bail.

By the time he got back to Torrington, officials there knew about what happened down the road in Nebraska. He was dismissed from his Police Judge position. His parish began the procedures to have him removed as their pastor. Minort's life was as good as over. The townspeople had a field day with the gossip of the horny minister, preaching on the pulpit on a Sunday morning, only to be having unlawful sexual carnal knowledge a few hours later.

The Reverend's wife had enough of his dalliances. Small towns are notorious for everyone knowing each other's business and gossip about the preacher was an ongoing subject around town. She told him that she would commit suicide, rather than continue being humiliated by him.

The air was crisp on the high plains of Wyoming on November 14, 1926. It was the first Sunday since his arrest and Minort had to face his congregation in a few hours. He was sure the men would snicker, while their wives elbowed their husbands in the pew. The church elders had already gotten the paperwork sent out to replace him. He felt hat his problems with the Mann Act were a political dirty trick. Now his ministry, his political career and his marriage was ruined. He had been effectively taken out of commission, thrown to the scrap heaps where fallen ministers go. He would be lucky to minister at a soup kitchen in Butte, Montana.

He looked at his long-suffering wife, whose first name is never mentioned, sleeping in the predawn darkness. Minort decided that he had to make things right, so he shot his sleeping wife with his shotgun.

Eleven-year old Herbert, hearing the blast ran into his parent's bedroom where he was gunned down by his father with a .45 caliber revolver. Minort briskly marched to the children's bedroom and shot five-year old LaVon, seven-year old David and ten-year old Clarence. David and Clarence were sound asleep when they were shot.

The Reverend washed up and got dressed. He sat at his kitchen table and wrote the following letter.

To the Public: -

I answered an urgent call to perform a wedding forty-eight miles southwest. On my way my radiator gave me trouble. Met two cars east of Henry, When I reached Henry, I decided to have the radiator repaired or get a taxi to take me over there. Two men at the point of a gun forced me to enter a car and was driven to Bayard under the same pressure, forced to register as man and wife. Twice I tried to get away and twice the gunmen were there. The woman in the case seemed to be an unwilling instrument to it all. No immorality was indulged in. About eleven o'clock officers appeared and later left. About one o'clock they returned (all the time I believed them part of the gang) and suggested if I would plead guilty to disturbing the peace I would be fined lightly and be allowed to return home. Seeing this the only way out, I agreed.

It was agreed that the matter wouldn't be published unless I could find out was at the bottom of it all. One of the men having a gun in sight at times was – who at one-time lived-in Torrington, he no doubt could shed light on it all.

I am sorry that this came out before I had time to sift it down. All I have found out was that _____ furnished the brains, with the help of one _____ and_____. It was my intention to have these men dealt with, but things have happened too quick and I was waiting to spend Sunday (today) to bring them to justice.
I must again in the face of very death swear that the whole thing was a well-prepared trap and frame. But thank God I am now beyond the power of such hellish human friends.

(Signed) B.J. Minort

He also wrote a letter to his son John who was living in Liberty Missouri, attending Bible College at William Jewell College. In a shaky hand, he wrote the following.

A revolver beckons me to use that, as I have used it on my loved ones. Strange all this should happen on Sunday morning as I was to preach on "Breaking the Alabaster Box." Goodbye! You have been a model son. No man has had a better set of children or a more faithful wife. (Signed) Your Dad-Loving you unto the end.

Minort telephoned local undertaker W.B. Longwith and asked him to come over to his house. The preacher picked up his big revolver and blew out his brains. He left a note for the authorities that his belongings should all be sold, his debts paid, and the rest of the money was to go to his son John. He requested that the family be buried in a single grave without a casket.

Was Reverend Minort telling the truth? Torrington is only five miles from the Nebraska state line. The Reverend was a two-state threat. His pro-labor Democratic politics cause concern among the politically conservative big farmers and ranchers who depended on cheap labor to run their extensive holdings. His name was grumbled in statehouses from Cheyenne to Lincoln.

Perhaps a simple, yet elaborate plan was set with only a few in the know. Ruin Minort's reputation and standing in the community, and problem solved. The cattlemen and farmers had plenty of money to hire the right men, and to pay off the proper officials. A little more than thirty years earlier the same men or their fathers hired their own army to threaten, beat or kill homesteaders in the Johnson County War. They probably did not expect that the Reverend would slaughter his family.

Perhaps the Reverend, being a passionate man about his faith, with honest redemption over his past, had a weakness for the female flesh? He was a charismatic speaker and had a congregation who came from miles around to hear his sermons. He had five children and a tired spouse who undoubtable kept the family home together while her husband ran around giving political speeches and tending his flock.

My conclusion is that the Reverend was a naïve and sensitive man, who firmly believed in his convictions, and his interpretation of the bible according to the Baptist Church. He had a weakness for the opposite sex, which was exploited by a group of politicians and landowners to stifle his influence with the local Democratic Party, and to humiliate him in front of his congregation.

Me and the Farmer

October 30, 1926
Mitchellville, Iowa
Murderer – William Boyd
Victim – Deputy Dewey Marshall

William Boyd was a half Cherokee/African American trying to scratch out a living as a farmer outside of Mitchellville, Iowa. He leased the old Kelley-Murrow farm about a half mile out of town. He lived most of his life two-hundred and fifty miles to the south in Sedalia, Missouri, and had only moved his wife and nine children to Mitchellville earlier in the year. Boyd bragged he had done very well for himself as a farmer back in the Show-Me State, but according to the sheriff of Pettis County, Missouri, Boyd had moved out of state to avoid prosecution for stealing hogs.

On October 30, 1926, Pettis County sheriff deputy's Grover Brent arrived from Missouri with a warrant for Boyd's arrest. Sheriff Findley assigned Deputy Dewey Marshall to accompany the visiting lawman. Checking in with Mitchellville's justice of the peace, the lawmen were informed that Boyd had papered the town with bad checks and many merchants had started legal steps for payment.

The story goes into two directions as this point. According to Boyd, he was sleeping in the bedroom with his infant. His wife and one of their older daughters had taken the interurban train to Des Moines to take care of some business. He was awoken by broken glass, and worried about the active Ku Klux Klan in Iowa grabbed his shotgun.

The children were screaming, and in the confusion, he did not realize that Marshall was a police officer. He shot the deputy in the head with a shotgun. Spotting Deputy Brent through a window, he shot him three times. Boyd ran out of his home and into the endless Iowa cornfields.

The official version of the incident is much more plausible. Boyd sent his wife and a daughter to Des Moines to sell some items and retrieve funds, so they could slip out of Mitchellville before their creditors knew. Boyd knew that the law was closing in on him and it was time to put some distance between him and the American Midwest. The children alerted their father to the police officers walking up to the kitchen door. As Deputy Marshall stepped onto the porch, Boyd fired one shot through the screen door, less than two feet from Marshall's head, killing him instantly.

Kicking open the shredded screen door, Boyd fired seven times at Deputy Brent, who was only a few steps behind Marshall. Boyd was hit in the eye, arm and leg, but survived. Nearby, farmers Alton Hart and T.J. Crawford were harvesting corn. They heard the shootout and saw Boyd toss the shotgun and grab the dead officer's pistol before he ran off to the field.

The police arrived and within the hour had surrounded the farmhouse while eight of Boyd's children cowered in the barn. Boyd's eleven-year old son, Homer, sobbed as he told the police, "Papa fired the shot."

Not taking Hart and Crawford at their word, the police believed that Boyd was still in the house. After tossing three cans of tear gas into the home, the police open fired on the home peppering it with bullet holes. Upon entering what was left of the house, police found out the children and the farmers were telling the truth. Boyd had escaped. Police took note that the home was filthy, with dirty dishes and clothing scattered all over the house. Items were also packed, as if they family were going to leave.

As police were going through their belongings, Mrs. Boyd and daughter were arrested on a Des Moines streetcar. She had cashed some worthless checks to raise money for their getaway. Police jailed her and put all the children in the county orphanage. Roadblocks were set up; a posse was organized, and bloodhounds were set out to find the cop killer.

Hysteria abounded as Iowans locked their doors and loaded their guns. Every light-skinned African American or dark-skinned Caucasian in the Des Moines metropolitan area was suspect, and the police were kept busy chasing calls from panic-stricken housewives and frantic farmers.

112

Authorities suspected that local African Americans were harboring Boyd. Black leaders and ministers were asked to spread the word in the community that Boyd was not to be protected.

Police in Missouri poured pressure on Boyd's relatives to give him up. After eight days on the lam, Boyd surrendered to the Polk County sheriff with his African American attorney, Charles Howard at his side.

The trial started on November 22, during an extreme cold spell with sub-zero temperatures, but the courtroom in Des Moines was packed with spectators, many of them African Americans. Polk County Attorney Vernon Seeburger opened the trial by calling the crime the most "bloodthirsty, blood curdling, diabolical murder of a law enforcement officer in history."

The jury of seven women and five men settled in for a poignant trial. The prosecution laid out a timeline of the events that led up to the murder of Deputy Dewey Marshall, and near fatal shooting of Deputy Grover Brent that Saturday morning in October. Seeburger brought up the charges of hog stealing from Sedalia as the reason why Boyd moved his family to Polk County.

Showing up in Mitchellville earlier in the year from Sedalia, Missouri with his wife and nine children, Boyd rented out the old Kelley-Murrow farm. He bought everything that he needed for spring planting from the merchants of Michellville, on credit, but he made enemies quickly in the small town outside of Des Moines, when the merchants discovered that Boyd's checks bounced like a tennis ball.

. Two days before the shooting, T. Mason of nearby Altoona brought a team of workmen to repossess thirty-five hogs that Boyd had bought with a bad check. Mason testified that Boyd was "in a sinister and threatening mood," during the retrieval. Mason told the court that Boyd had stated, "I'll kill someone if they keep pinching me on those bad checks."

Seeburger paraded every person that he could to testify for the prosecution, including the still bandaged Deputy Grover Brent, who came the two hundred-thirty miles from Sedalia and eye-witnesses Hart and Crawford. The most powerful witness was William Boyd's eleven-year-old son, Homer.

113

The December 1, 1926 Ames Daily Tribune led the story with the headline, "Own Son's Story May Send Negro Killer to Rope," and went on to describe Homer as "a little brown boy."

William Boyd took the stand and gave his version of shootouts. He stuck to his story that he had been sleeping when he heard the children scream that there was a man in the house, and that he had shot the deputies in self-defense, believing that they were Klansmen. Boyd could not explain why his wife was in Des Moines cashing bad checks and selling valuable items. He denied that the family was packed up and ready to slip out of Michellville unnoticed. He stated that he was afraid of racist Ku Klux Klan members in the village of Michellville and told the court that his children were harassed at school by racist children.

In his closing argument the always dramatic Vernon Seeburger did his best to reduce Boyd to the level of a wild beast exclaiming, "He has the movements of a panther and the cunning of a fox and is surrounded by a devil complex." He demanded the death penalty for Boyd.

The Sedalia Capital newspaper printed the headline, "Quadroon Stoic as Jury Declares Fate," and The Ames Daily Tribune wrote, "Negro Battles on Witness Stand to Save Neck from Noose – Sticks to Story thru Severe Examination." Central Iowa held its collective breath while the jury deliberated.

On December 14, 1926, while the temperature outside sat below zero, the jury decided on their fourth ballot to find William Boyd guilty, and sentenced him to life in prison. All nine of the Boyd children were put into orphanages.

Just a Good Old Boy

December 1st and 5th, 1926

Farwell, Texas

Murderer - George Jefferson Hassell

Victims – Suzie Hassell / Alton Hassell / Sammie Hassell / David Hassell

Maude Hassell / John Hassell / Virgil Hassell / Marie Vogel and her three

adopted children

The panhandle of Texas is a desolate place. The flat, arid high plains were once the southernmost range of the American Bison. Before the invasion of the Europeans this southern edge of the Western High Plains was described as a Sea of Grass. Later it was called the Great American Desert. It was the land of the Apache, until the Comanche got their horses from the Spanish invaders and chased them into two directions - west into New Mexico and east into Oklahoma.

Parmer County, Texas sits perfectly square at the bottom left of the Texas Panhandle. Its western boundary abuts New Mexico like a stranger on a crowded bus. There are only three towns in Parmer County; Bovina, Friona and the county seat, Farwell. Parmer County is a dry county, which may be the reason that only ten-thousand people live in this visually tedious land. Apart from a tornado, or an extremely cold winter, nothing much has happened in Parmer County, except in 1926.

George Jefferson Hassell was born in Smithville Texas on July 25, 1888, the youngest of seven children he was called Jeffie by his family. His mother was a fundamentalist Christian and was strict with her children about obeying the Ten Commandments, but that did not stop Hassell from breaking every single one during his life, starting with getting caught stealing tobacco at the age of seven. Later in life, Hassell claimed to have started using tobacco at six-years old and lost his virginity at the tender age of eight, to a fifteen-year old girl.

115

The family moved to Oklahoma in 1898, where Jeffie's mother died in April 1901. His father quickly remarried and by November Jeffie left home. The thirteen-year old roamed the high plains working on farms and ranches.

When George found out that his father died in 1905, he believed that his stepmother had poisoned him. He went back to Oklahoma to seek revenge. Unfortunately, he funded his trip with a sizeable bank deposit that his boss had trusted him to drop at a bank. Instead of murdering his stepmother and her children, George got drunk and passed out near her home.

A few days later, George went back to the ranch and talked his boss into dropping the charges and let him work off the money that he stole. But the state of Texas felt otherwise and prosecuted the seventeen-year old. He was found guilty and sentenced to two years in prison.

The same day that Hassell was released from prison, he enlisted in the United States Army. Because he did not want his criminal record discovered, he used his mother's maiden name. Hassell lasted nine months before he got into a fight with a cook and deserted.

He drifted to Abilene, Texas where he met Minnie Lofley, a fine young lady whom he swept off her feet and married against her family's wishes. A son was born, however that did nothing to endear him to Minnie's family. Citing interference from her relatives, Hassell left town and his family after two years.

Hassell was a big man with an affable personality. He was what is now called, "a good old boy," a country rube, who was smarter and more cunning than he led people to believe. He was a good worker, who got along well with the lower members of society, particularly the more criminal minded. He drank, and told amusing stories, but he never stayed anywhere for long.

For unknown reasons, Hassell joined the United States Navy, but soon deserted his post in San Francisco. Making his way back to Texas, and the family that he left behind, but got as far as Fresno when he decided that army life suited him better. His identity was quickly discovered, and he was sentenced to two years at Mare Island Naval Base near San Francisco. He finished up his sentence

116

at Fort Leavenworth and was released to the custody of the Navy to face desertion charge. He was sentenced to one year in prison in Norfolk, Virginia.

When he was released from prison, he hot footed it to Winters, Texas where he heard Minnie and their son was living. Their reunion did not go as Hassell planned. Minnie wanted nothing to do with Hassell. His four-year old son threw rocks at him while yelling at him to get lost.

Dejected, Hassell once again hit the road. From this point on Hassell's life is even sketchier than it was before. He claimed to have lived and worked in thirty-seven states and had cohabitated with at least seven women and had married another. He earned a living being a ranch hand, oil rigger, miner and merchant mariner. When times were tough, he and his girl would pull the "Badger Game," on an unwary businessman.

The Badger Game is a blackmail scam in which an attractive woman picks up a man of means, seduces him, and gets him into a sexually compromising situation when her partner, posing as her husband barges in on the couple. They threaten to inform his wife or employer what happened, hence ruining his life if he does not pay.

While waiting New Orleans for a ship to be assigned to him, Hassell received news that his brother had been kicked in the head by a mule on his farm on July 1, 1924. His brother's widow, Suzie, asked if he could come out to their farm to help with the harvest. They were married four months later in Farwell, Texas on October 8, 1924.

George and Suzie, along with her brood of eight children ranging from two to twenty-one years old lived on a dirt farm about five miles east of Farwell, where they eked out a living on the arid high plains. George integrated himself into the community with his friendly backslapping ways, and all was well on the farm.

In 1925, Suzie's oldest daughter, her husband and two children came to visit from California. Unbeknown to everyone, George had visited his niece, his brother's child a few years before while she was separated from her husband. The

117

affair resulted in a child. Sometime during the visit their passions reignited, causing much ado on the farm. The visitors departed, and Suzie's attitude to the man that she married changed. She never had sex with her him again.

December 1, 1926 was a balmy day with temperatures in the low seventies during the day. Twenty-one-year-old Alton was working off the farm for the week, earning some money by mowing hay. George finished his day by drinking a pint of whiskey in the barn. Smelling the liquor on his breath, Suzie got angry and words were exchanged. George lost his composure, and clobbered Suzie with a ballpeen hammer. Before he knew it, his meaty hands were around the woman's throat strangling the last bit of life out of her. Two-year old Sammie was screaming, so George strangled the little boy to death.

Sneaking into their bedrooms Hassell proceeded to strangle, fourteen-year old Maude, seven-year old David, and six-year old Johnny. Eighteen-year old Virgil and twelve-year old Russell were not so easy to kill. During the struggle Hassell got hit in the head with a brick. Hassell put an end to the battle by picking up an axe, leaving the brothers a mutilated mess.

Alton was not expected home until Saturday, which gave Hassell plenty of time to clean up. He dug a hole along the side of the house and filled it with the dead bodies of his family.

Alton arrived a day late on a rainy and sleety Sunday evening. Hassell told him that since the crop was in, his mother and siblings went to visit Aunt Liddy in Shallowater, eighty miles to the southeast.

Exhausted from a week of threshing, Alton collapsed in his bed. Hassell waited an hour or two, took a swig of whiskey and blasted Alton's head off with a shotgun. Alton took his place in the communal grave he now shared with his family members.

Hassell kept the farm going as if his wife and family were off visiting Aunt Liddy in Shallowater. He told friends and neighbors that they were giving up farming and Suzie and the kids had already moved to their new home in Oklahoma. He was going to tie up some loose ends and sell off their tools and equipment.

On December 23, Hassell had his moving sale. Items sold briskly as Hassell backslapped and made sale pitches. Not everyone at the sale was there to buy. Sheriff Martin of Parmer County was there too, and he never quite trusted Hassell. He recognized an ex-con when he saw one, and the story of his family just packing up and moving in December smelled funny to him.

A loaded wagon pulled by a mule rolled directly over the pit where the bodies were buried, sinking to the axle. While trying to lift the wagon, the men saw blood-soaked blankets. George grabbed a knife and stabbed himself but was quickly subdued by the crowd.

Sheriff Martin was worried that a lynching would happen if Hassell was housed in the Parmer County Jail, so every available deputy in three counties escorted Hassell to the hospital in Plainview. Once he was stitched up, he was taken to the jail in Lubbock.

Gertrude Hoffman saw the photo of the smiling Hassell in a Pittsburgh newspaper. She called Sheriff Martin and told him that she recognized Hassell as G.G. Baker, a man who was allegedly married to her sister Marie Vogel. She had last seen her sister in 1917, in Whittier, California. Later that year she received an odd letter written by Baker informing her that Marie, along with her three adopted children had moved to Australia. The Pittsburgh woman did not believe him, she knew Baker had killed them.

Hassell had already admitted his guilt in the Farwell murders and happily sat in his jail cell waiting for his trial when he was asked if he had even lived in Whittier, California. The murderer admitted he had, and he had killed his family in 1917, burying them under the house they shared.

Sheriff Martin called authorities in California informing them about Hassell's story. The murderer could not remember the exact address of the home, so he drew a map, which was mailed to Los Angeles County Sheriff's Department. Initially, the L.A. Sheriffs were annoyed with tip, believing that some rube in Texas was just delaying his date with the electric chair. In 1926, Whittier was a small ranching town of eight-thousand people and finding the house at 7241 S. Whittier Avenue was a simple matter. There were still some neighbors around who remembered the couple. They told police that around the time that the family disappeared they saw Hassell moving dirt from under his house, and they had complained to him about the rank odor coming from the property.

Police found the skeleton of Marie Vogel, and the bones of an eight-year old boy, a five-year old girl and an infant boy buried under the home.

Hassell told authorities that he had killed them all on the day the United States declared war on Germany, April 6, 1917. Hassell, was working as a hand on a ranch owned by a doctor, and shared a home with Marie Vogel, who worked for the same doctor as a housekeeper. Hassell was not sure if they were legally married, but they had adopted three children who were orphans from Pittsburgh. Upset that the country was at war, Hassell wanted to join the military to fight for his country. Marie thought his idea was ridiculous. He was twenty-nine years old and had three children. He was needed at home. Hassell strangled her to death, and then systematically strangled the children. He buried them under the house before he left town.

When asked why he had killed two wives, and eleven children, Hassell explained. "No one ever lived who loved children more than I did. If you can tell me why I killed her and those children or why I killed again at Farwell I will give my life before my execution day – and die satisfied."

The trial was quick. Hassell admitted to the murders and was tried on one count of murder for the killing of Alton. He was escorted to Huntsville Prison where he was put on death row. Authorities in California decided not to extradite him to face charges in the murders of Marie Vogel and her three children.

Hassell spent over a year on death row while the case was appealed. Prison life seemed to agree with Hassell. He was chatty and good natured with guards, reporters and other prisoners. He ate heartedly, and was a model prisoner, who had a calming effect on his fellow inmates. The murderer accepted his fate and was happy to discuss his thoughts. He told a guard that his last twelve months in custody were the best years of his life. "I had plenty to eat," he said, "and nobody to bother me."

The following are some of his better quotes.

I don't look like a murderer; I don't act like a bad man. I loved and respected the children and the women I killed.

Some of my forefathers may have hanged by the neck, but none of them hung by tails.

Life is sweet even if it is in a jail. I don't believe in Hell or Heaven.

I think I have served my hell on Earth. If God is just, he'll not kick me off into fire and brimstone.

I'm a lot luckier than you are," he told a reporter. "You don't know what day you will get run over by a car, get shot or how long you will live suffering from a lingering illness while I know exactly when I will die. We both know we have to die sometime. I am protected and I am being fattened before my final day.

Hassell did not want the cooks to make any fuss and declined to order a special last dinner. He ate what was being served that day; bacon, fried potatoes, stewed prunes, baked beans, coffee, milk and toast. Two women, believed to be Hassell's sisters, as well as a cousin came to the prison during his final days. The warden did not allow Hassell to see them.

During his final hour, Hassell asked Robert Lee Benton, an African American who was also scheduled to be executed that day, if he wanted to go first. Benton replied, "Mr. George, you know a white man always goes before a Negro."

A little past midnight on February 10, 1928, Hassell was led from his cell on Huntsville's death row and taken to the execution room. He looked out at the twenty-five spectators, all of whom were reporters or law enforcement personnel. The warden asked if he had anything to say. Composed, but slightly trembling, George Jefferson Hassell looked at the assembled crowd and said, "I would like to announce to the world that I am prepared to meet my God. I have made my confession to God and Man. Man does not understand it all, but God does."

The electric chair at Huntsville Prison was first used in 1924. Handcrafted by convicts and nicknamed "Old Sparky." It was used until 1964 and three-hundred-sixty-two people died by it.

At 12:22A.M., Hassell got his first jolt of electricity. Two more jolts followed and Hassell was declared dead at 12:29 A.M. Robert Lee Benton was executed in 'Old Sparky" an hour later. Hassell was the thirty-seventh person to be executed by electrocution in Texas and the fifth white man send to his maker by "Old Sparky."

The Nebraska Traveler Assassination

December 17, 1926
Leigh, Nebraska
Murderer – Ted Mason
Victim - Fame Shafer

Leigh, Nebraska lays eighty-six miles northwest of Omaha and ninety miles southeast of Lincoln, deep in the lilting Nebraskan farmland. It would seem to be the last place where you would find a gypsy camp.

The Mason family were travelers, part of the Gypsy culture which came over from the British Isles any way they could. Travelers make a living by many means, some are honest, some are con artists, and all of them spend much of the year on the road.

Sixty-year old Frank Mason was the leader of his clan. Their family made their living in the horse-trading business. Although the United State had plenty of automobiles and trucks in 1926, there was still a demand for buying, selling and trading horses throughout the central plains. The Mason family worked a circuit during the spring and summer traveling throughout the Plains states and wintered in the low hills outside of Leigh, Nebraska. They traveled and lived in an ornate and expensive horse drawn wagon. The matriarch of the Mason family died the year before, leaving the clan emotionally broken and Frank a widower.

Frank's twenty-year old son, Duffy married a non-traveler, eighteen-year old Fame Shafer on April 17, 1926. Famie, as she was known was a local girl who lived in Schuyler, the county seat of Colfax County. Like the Masons, her family was in the horseflesh business, and although not Travelers, the families knew each other well. She was described as having a zest for life. The marriage lasted one day.

Instead of going back to her family after her disastrous wedding night, Famie stayed with the Mason family and became especially close to Frank, much to the displeasure of most of the clan.

123

Travelers take care of their business their own way, without courts, and with great secrecy. The tension built throughout the summer traveling season, and once back at the winter camp outside of Leigh things did not improve. Hattie Stevens, one of Famie's sister in-laws impulsively stabbed Famie in the shoulder. A few days later, Frank's son Ted yelled at Famie for daring to use his mother's old cooking utensils, telling her that she was not worthy of touching anything of his mother's.

Most people would get the hint and find a different place to spend the winter, but Famie was headstrong, and Frank insisted that she stay. While the cold snap that hit the Midwest in December 1926 was keeping everyone inside, Frank and Famie took a jaunt to Omaha for a few days. It was good to get away from the clan and their close quarters they shared. The pair stayed at a downtown hotel, signing in as father and daughter, and spent their time shopping and exploring the city.

When the couple got back to Leigh on December 17th, they visited Thorps Barbershop in the center of the village. Famie wanted her hair cut into a bob, which was a daring fashion statement in 1926, and Frank was happy to pay for it.

As Famie sat in the barber chair, being attended by barber C. L. Thorpe, when Duffy and his older brother Ted entered the shop. Ted stepped behind the wannabe flapper and shot her in the back of her head. The bullet entered the base of her skull and lodged in her forehead. Famie fell into Frank's arms and died in about ten minutes.

For some reason, Duffy threw his hat and coat onto the floor and shouted, "My brother and I are not afraid! We won't run!" Then the men left the barbershop, Ted firing a celebratory shot into the air.

The men walked across the street to August Koppel's Pool Hall and Soft Drink Parlor. Ted brandished his pistol and shouted, "I've just killed a woman!" Duffy meekly asked Koppel to call the town marshal. Just as any proprietor of a prohibition era "Soft Drink" parlor Koppel refused.

The pair were eventually arrested peacefully and taken to the Colfax County jail in Schuyler. Frank came right away to see if he could do anything for his sons and a heated argument broke out between father and sons. Frank got tired of the drama asked the marshal to give Ted a gun, adding, "to see if he's got the nerve enough to finish me off." To which Ted responded, "I don't want to shoot you. If I had wanted to kill you, I could have done it long ago."

The brothers did not enter a plea when they were arraigned in court. Their attorney entered a not guilty plea and asked for separate trials.

Ted's trial started on February 24, 1927 and was over two days later. There were four witnesses to the murder, and although Frank and barber C. L. Thorpe could not say for certain who had fired the pistol into young woman's brain, the testimony of barber Tedford Busse and his brother Elmer, as well as "Soft Drink" parlor operator August Koppel sealed Ted's fate. Ted was sentenced to life in prison.

The charges against Duffy were dropped on March 10, 1927. Duffy told the press that he never wanted to marry Famie, but was forced to by Frank, so they could be closer without causing an uproar over their forty-two-year age disparity. He also blamed his father, who would not allow his children to go to school for his ignorance and illiteracy.

Duffy left the Travelers life, got an education and became a farmer.

Thy Brother's Keeper

December 23, 1926
South Salon, Ohio
Murderer – Leo Halterman
Victims – Charles Halterman / Carrie Halterman

Leo Halterman was a millennium baby, a twin, born at the beginning of the Twentieth Century on a farm near the Pike County village of Beaver, Ohio. The rugged farm country taught life lessons early.

Leo Halterman had been accident prone from a young age. When he was a pre-teen, he was kicked in the stomach by a horse. Later he was kicked by a cow and broke his leg. After he was run over by a horse driven cargo wagon, he stopped growing. He was only four-foot-eight-inches tall and never weighed more than one-hundred and twenty pounds.

His accident saved him from being drafted during World War I, and since the Spanish Flu tended to kill the fit, Leo was ducking death like a high heeled devil. Like most young men of rural upbringing, Leo left school to work by his early teenage years. He worked at a drug store and a steel plant for a time. He got a job building farm machines in Peoria, where once again, the accident-prone man got caught between two moving pieces of steel. He suffered injuries to his hips and spinal cord. He was in a full body cast for six months and had to endure several more corrective operations afterwards.

Despite his bad luck and small stature, Leo got married in 1921 to Garnet Thornton, moved to Portsmouth, Ohio and got a job as a fireman on a railroad. By 1924, they had three children, daughter Joan and twins William and James.

Leo suddenly quit the railroad in 1925, left his family, and moved back to central Ohio, but things were not the same back home. His parents had divorced, and his mother and twin-sister Cleo had moved away. His father had a new family. A couple of his couple of brothers had their own farms. His kinfolk did not take

126

kindly that he abandoned his family. His twenty-two-year-old stepbrother Charles called him a "damn fool."

Leo left Pike County and for unknown reason went to Windsor, Ontario, Canada where he worked as a waiter for a short time, before ending up working at a steel plant in Sandusky, Ohio. Having abandoned his family, a warrant went out for the twenty-six-year old's arrest.

Stepbrother Charles, who was married, but childless went off in search of his older half-brother and found him in Sandusky. He told Leo that if he went back to Portsmouth, Ohio, his wife's hometown, he would not be arrested. Leo traveled to the old Ohio River town and was promptly arrested for abandonment. Charles, who was called Chas, paid his five hundred-dollar bail on the conditions that Leo lived and worked on Chas's farm on Blessing Crossing Road, near South Salon, ninety miles northwest of Portsmouth.

Chas and his wife Carrie treated Leo like a slave. Leo was not allowed to be in the house if Carrie was home. He had to live in an outbuilding, not much better than the farm animals. He was also not allowed to receive mail from his wife. Chas would throw letters into the furnace, right in front of Leo. Chas slapped, punched and kicked his tiny brother for the slightest mistakes. Chas cupped Leo on the head for stopping for supper at a neighbor's home while hauling grain to market. He beat him for accidently letting a sow escape from her pen. Not long after Leo's arrival at the hell farm, his twin sons, William and James arrived from Portsmouth. Their mother, Garnet could not take care of them and her daughter at the same time.

Chas and Carrie adored the boys and would not allow Leo to be with them unsupervised. Once while sawing lumber, Chas hit Leo across the side of his face with a stick of wood because Leo cautioned his children away from the saw.

Leo managed to receive a letter from Garnet. She wanted to visit that Thanksgiving. When Leo told Chas, he angrily told them that he cannot invite anyone to his home. Leo wrote a letter back, but Chas intercepted it and threw it in a fire. Carrie and Chas did not want the twins to see their mother. The

127

next day Chas got so angry at Leo that he chased him with his shotgun. He would have killed him had Carrie not stopped him.

On a cold Monday evening on December 20, 1926, the siblings went at it again. Apparently, Leo was given five dollars to buy Christmas presents and spent the money on alcohol. Someone in South Salon saw Leo drinking and telephoned Chas. He angrily went out to catch him and once he got ahold of his slightly built brother, he beat, slapped and kicked him down the icy and muddy street. This time there were non-family witnesses to the violence, and they all heard Leo scream, "You'll be sorry for this!"

In the early morning hours of December 23, 1926, Leo woke up Chas telling him that he thought he heard someone creeping around outside. They had been recently plagued by chicken thieves, so Chas bolted out of bed and ran outside. Leo was right behind him and once they reached the chicken coops, Leo grabbed a double-barreled shotgun he had stashed and shot his abusive brother in the back. Although Chas was dead, Leo fired the second shell point-blank into the side of his head.

Hearing to gunshot, Carrie ran out of the house and seeing Chas lying on the ground, dead, she attacked her brother in-law with her fists. Leo, out of ammo, used the shotgun as a club, beating his sister in-law until it broke apart. Retrieving a hatchet, Leo hacked the prone woman until she was not recognizable.

Ditching the shotgun and the hatchet in an abandoned well, Leo cleaned up and got word out to the police that something terrible had happened on the farm. When the police arrived, they were stunned by the murder scene. Chas had been shot in the back at close range and there was little left of his head. Carrie had between eight to ten gashed in her head. There was evidence that at one point, the hatchet was buried in her brain. The broken shotgun was found in the old well. The gore covered hatchet was in a nearby shed, as was Leo's bloody clothes.

Leo blamed former farmhand Sam Satterfield for the murders. Leo told police that his brother had recently fired Satterfield and that he threatened revenge.

Skeptical of the tale, police picked up Satterfield and took Leo into custody as a witness.

Satterfield was soon release from detention when his alibi was found to be true and all the evidence pointed to Leo. Police then turned on Leo for answers and the slight man caved to the police like a child's snow fort in March. With the promise that he would not be executed, Leo Halterman told the prosecutors what happened that cold morning.

The trial started on February 14, 1927, with Judge C.A. Reid and much to Halterman's dismay the prosecution asked for the death penalty. When Halterman's defense attorney's B.F. Friedman, Pope Greg and Judge A.C. Patton objected, the prosecution told the court they had promised Halterman nothing.

The trial went on for a week and was the hottest ticket in western Ohio. Extra police had to be called in to control the crowd as hundreds of people were turned away from the standing room only courtroom. Women were touched with emotion when Leo's mother and Cleo arrived at the courtroom and warmly embraced him.

On February 21, 1927, the prosecution introduced Kenneth Anderson, an eighteen-year old African American. On the stand Anderson testified that on Monday, December 20, 1926, the day that Leo spent five dollars getting drunk instead of buying Christmas presents, Leo Halterman offered him fifty dollars to shoot his half-brother and wife.

The Washington Courthouse Herald wrote: "Anderson made a good witness. He answered the questions with typical Negro boy answers. He did not seem confused or nervous on the stand. And he gave the spectators several good laughs."

In his cross-examination defense attorney Judge A.C. Patton doubted Anderson's story by asking the jury, "who ever heard of a coon standing outside like a black spot on the wall on a cold December night?" The racist attorney also brought up Anderson's previous brushes with the law.

Stepbrother Bert Halterman got on the stand. Bert lived on his own farm just down the road from his brother's. He testified honestly and without malice. He told the jury how Chas paid Leo, forty dollars a month, with ten dollars going to Garnet, ten to Leo and twenty dollars going back to Chas for taking care of Leo and the twins. He testified that Chas and Carrie had been kind to the twins and mentioned adopting them.

Carrie Halterman's niece, twenty-three-year old teacher Constance Hammerstein testified on December 20, 1926, while visiting her aunt, she witnessed the fight between Leo and Chas. She testified that she heard Leo yell out to Chas, "You'll be sorry for this." She said that there was no blood on him, nor did he have a black eye.

Burt Halterman's son, Floyd told the jury Leo asked him to tell the police he had been at a pool hall and heard Sam Satterfield say that he was going to kill Charles and Carrie. Shortly before the dual homicide, Leo told Floyd, "something is going to happen and that if you don't stick by me and they send me to the penitentiary, I'll shoot you when I get out." The defense responded by asking Floyd multiplication questions, as how many feet are in a mile.

The defense brought out a dozen character witnesses who all had good things to say about the killer, although none of them had been in contact with him in over five years. His mother took the stand and told the story of Leo's sicknesses, and suffering. How when he was fourteen, he had been run over by a wagon and had never grown any bigger. She broke down crying several times. When the prosecution cross-examined her, she was guarded with her answers and did not volunteer any more information than she was asked.

Leo Halterman took the witness stand in his defense and was his own worst witness. He told of his life of illnesses, and injuries. How he was abused by people because of his short height and slight of build. He went into full detail about the night of the murders, telling the prosecutor he shot his brother in the head, "because I knew that if I hadn't killed him, he'd kill me." He added that everything went black while he killed Carrie. He sunk his own ship with his testimony.

After twenty-three hours of deliberation, the jury came back with verdict of guilty, and Leo Halterman was sentenced to die in the electric chair at the Ohio Penitentiary in Columbus.

On June 17, 1927, Leo Halterman was led to the execution chamber at 8:50p.m. Because of his short stature, the prison guards had to set up blocks for his feet because they could not reach the floor.

Before he was hooked up, Halterman announced to the attendees, "tone walls and iron bars my keep people out of this place but not the spirit of Jesus Christ. I want to say to you that Jesus Christ came down within these walls to me and washed my sins away and I am going to meet him. I forgive all and I will be waiting for you at the Golden Gate. I hope to meet you one and all there."

At 8:55p.m., the power was turned on and Halterman was dead in three minutes. He was taken to his mother's home near Salem, Ohio, where he had an open casket wake. So many people showed up that not all of them got to see his fried body.

The Circleville Daily Union Herald's headline on June 17, 1926 was "Lilliputian Murderer is Electrocuted."

Bibliography

Abilene Daily Reporter

Abilene Morning Reporter-News

Ada Evening News

Afton Star Valley Independent

Albert Lea Evening Tribune

Alton Evening Telegraph

Altoona Herald

Amarillo Sunday News Globe

Ames Daily Tribune

Ames Evening Times

Anderson Herald Bulletin

Anniston Star

Ardmore Daily Ardmoreite

Atlantic News Telegraph

Augusta Chronicle

Battle Creek Enquirer

Beatrice Daily Sun

Bedford Times Republican

Berkeley Daily Gazette

Biddeford Daily Journal

Big Timbers Pioneer

Billings Gazette

Biloxi Daily Herald

Bradford Era

Brainerd Daily Dispatch

Brandon Daily Sun

Brownsville Herald

Burlington Gazette

Burlington Hawk Eye

Burnet Bulletin

Carbondale Daily Free Press

Cedar Valley Daily Times

Charleston Daily Mail

Chicago Daily Tribune

Chicago Tribune

Chillicothe Constitutional - Tribune

Cincinnati Enquirer

Circleville Daily Union Herald

The Circleville Herald

Corvallis Gazette-Times

 Coshocton Tribune

Creston Daily Advertiser

Cumberland Evening Times

Daily City News

Detroit Free Press

Detroit News

East Liverpool Review Tribune

Emporia Gazette

Escanaba Daily Press

Eufaula Indian Journal

The Evening Independent

Evening Independents

Fairfield Daily Ledger

Fayetteville Daily Democrat

Fitchburg Sentinel

Florence Morning News Review

Galveston Daily News

Glenwood Opinion

Grand Haven Tribune

Greensburg Daily News

Hamilton Evening Journal

Hammond Times

Harrison Times

Havre Daily News Promoter

Hattiesburg American

Helena Independent

Independent Helena Montana

The Indian Journal

Indiana Evening Gazette

Jefferson City Daily Capital

Joplin Globe

Journal Gazette Mattoon

Key West Citizen

Kingsport Times

Kokomo Tribune

La Crosse Tribune

La Crosse Tribune And Leader Press

Laredo Daily Times

Laurel Daily Leader

Lebanon Daily News And The Lebanon Daily
Times

Lewiston Evening Journal

Lincoln Star

Literary Digest

Logansport Press

Lowell Sun

Marysville Daily Democrat

Maryville Daily Democrat Forum

Miami Daily Arizona Silver Belt

Miami News Record

Moberly Monitor

Monroe News Star

Mount Pleasant Daily News

Murphysboro Daily Independent

Muscatine Journal And News Tribune

Newark American Tribune

The News – Frederick Maryland

New Castle Herald

The New Republic

North Adams Transcript

Oneonta Daily Star

Pinedale Roundup

Pittsburgh Daily Post

The Plattsmouth Journal

Portsmouth Herald

Quanah Tribune Chief

Republic City News

Salem News

San Antonio Express

St. Louis Post-Dispatch

Sarasota Herald-Tribune

Seattle Post-Intelligencer

Seattle Times

Sedalia Capital

Seymour Daily Tribune

Sheboygan Press

Springfield Leader

Springfield Union

The State Journal Lansing

Taylor Daily Press

Thomasville Daily Times Enterprise

Tampa Tribune

The Times Herald Port Huron

The Times Recorder

Tipton Tribune

Titusville Herald

Twin Falls Daily News

Tyrone Daily Herald

Ukiah Dispatch Democrat

Uniontown Morning Herald

Washington Courthouse Herald

Waterloo Evening Courier

Winona (Minn.) Daily News

Whittier Daily News

Zanesville Times Recorder

Author's Biography

Born to First Generation Americans in Bay City, Michigan.

David Kulczyk is the author of five California crime books. He has a B.A in History from California State University – Sacramento

Books by David Kulczyk

California Justice – Shootouts, Lynchings and Assassinations in the Golden State

Death In California – The Bizarre, Freakish, and Just Curious Ways People Die in the Golden State

California Fruits, Flakes and Nuts – True Tales of California Crazies, Crackpots and Creeps

California's Deadliest Women – Dangerous Dames and Murderous Moms.

Forgotten Sacramento Murders – 1940 - 1976

Calendar for year 1926 (United States)

January

Su	Mo	Tu	We	Th	Fr	Sa
					1	2
3	4	5	6	7	8	9
10	11	12	13	14	15	16
17	18	19	20	21	22	23
24	25	26	27	28	29	30
31						

7:◑ 14:● 20:◐ 28:○

February

Su	Mo	Tu	We	Th	Fr	Sa
	1	2	3	4	5	6
7	8	9	10	11	12	13
14	15	16	17	18	19	20
21	22	23	24	25	26	27
28						

5:◑ 12:● 19:◐ 27:○

March

Su	Mo	Tu	We	Th	Fr	Sa
	1	2	3	4	5	6
7	8	9	10	11	12	13
14	15	16	17	18	19	20
21	22	23	24	25	26	27
28	29	30	31			

7:◑ 13:● 21:◐ 29:○

April

Su	Mo	Tu	We	Th	Fr	Sa
				1	2	3
4	5	6	7	8	9	10
11	12	13	14	15	16	17
18	19	20	21	22	23	24
25	26	27	28	29	30	

5:◑ 12:● 19:◐ 27:○

May

Su	Mo	Tu	We	Th	Fr	Sa
						1
2	3	4	5	6	7	8
9	10	11	12	13	14	15
16	17	18	19	20	21	22
23	24	25	26	27	28	29
30	31					

4:◑ 11:● 19:◐ 27:○

June

Su	Mo	Tu	We	Th	Fr	Sa
		1	2	3	4	5
6	7	8	9	10	11	12
13	14	15	16	17	18	19
20	21	22	23	24	25	26
27	28	29	30			

3:◑ 10:● 18:◐ 25:○

July

Su	Mo	Tu	We	Th	Fr	Sa
				1	2	3
4	5	6	7	8	9	10
11	12	13	14	15	16	17
18	19	20	21	22	23	24
25	26	27	28	29	30	31

2:◑ 9:● 17:◐ 25:○ 31:◑

August

Su	Mo	Tu	We	Th	Fr	Sa
1	2	3	4	5	6	7
8	9	10	11	12	13	14
15	16	17	18	19	20	21
22	23	24	25	26	27	28
29	30	31				

8:● 16:◐ 23:○ 30:◑

September

Su	Mo	Tu	We	Th	Fr	Sa
			1	2	3	4
5	6	7	8	9	10	11
12	13	14	15	16	17	18
19	20	21	22	23	24	25
26	27	28	29	30		

7:● 15:◐ 21:○ 28:◑

October

Su	Mo	Tu	We	Th	Fr	Sa
					1	2
3	4	5	6	7	8	9
10	11	12	13	14	15	16
17	18	19	20	21	22	23
24	25	26	27	28	29	30
31						

6:● 14:◐ 21:○ 28:◑

November

Su	Mo	Tu	We	Th	Fr	Sa
	1	2	3	4	5	6
7	8	9	10	11	12	13
14	15	16	17	18	19	20
21	22	23	24	25	26	27
28	29	30				

5:● 12:◐ 19:○ 27:◑

December

Su	Mo	Tu	We	Th	Fr	Sa
			1	2	3	4
5	6	7	8	9	10	11
12	13	14	15	16	17	18
19	20	21	22	23	24	25
26	27	28	29	30	31	

5:● 12:◐ 19:○ 27:◑

Holidays and Observances:

Jan 1	New Year's Day	May 30 Decoration Day	Dec 24 'Christmas Day' observed
Feb 12 Lincoln's Birthday	Jun 20 Father's Day	Dec 24 Christmas Eve
Feb 14 Valentine's Day	Jul 4 Independence Day	Dec 25 Christmas Day
Feb 22 Presidents' Day	Sep 6 Labor Day	Dec 31 'New Year's Day' observed
Apr 4 Easter Sunday	Oct 31 Halloween	Dec 31 New Year's Eve
May 9 Mother's Day	Nov 25 Thanksgiving Day	

139

Made in the USA
San Bernardino, CA
25 July 2019